LOVE AND ROMANCE IN EARLY DRAMA

volume 54 | 2015

Copyright 2015 Mario Longtin

Published simultaneously in Canada.
Printed in the United States of America.

First Printing 2015
First Circle Publishing: London, Ontario, Canada
www.firstcirclepublishing.com

ISBN-13: 978-0-9919760-3-4
ISBN-10: 0991976037

ROMARD: Research on Medieval and Renaissance Drama
vol. 54 | 2015

Love and Romance in Early Drama

Guest Editors	Charlotte Steenbrugge
	Alexandra F. Johnston
Chief Editor	Mario Longtin

www.FirstCirclePublishing.com

The Medieval and Renaissance Drama Society (MRDS)

The Medieval and Renaissance Drama Society is an academic association of scholars, artists, and other individuals interested in Medieval and Renaissance drama. The Society's activities include organizing annual meetings, sponsoring long-range research projects, and publishing material of interest to the membership. The annual journal ROMARD, and the Early European Drama in Translation Series (EEDTS) are publications affiliated with MRDS. The MRDS business meeting is held annually each May at the International Congress on Medieval Studies at Western Michigan University in Kalamazoo, Michigan. Members and non-members are invited to attend. Each year MRDS sponsors conference sessions at the Medieval Congress in Kalamazoo, the Modern Language Association Convention, and the Medieval Congress in Leeds, England.

MRDS members receive the Society's Newsletter twice a year and the annual issue of ROMARD. To join MRDS, please visit the Society's website (http://mrds.eserver.org/) or contact the MRDS Secretary/Treasurer Carolyn Coulson-Grigsby at ccoulson2@su.edu. Dues Structure: Regular Member (US $25); Student (US $10); Friend (US $50); Benefactor (US $100).

About ROMARD

Guest Editors vol. 54	Charlotte Steenbrugge University of Toronto University of Bristol
	Alexandra F. Johnston University of Toronto
Chief Editor	Mario Longtin Western University, London, Ontario
Associate Editor	David Klausner University of Toronto
Copy Editor	M. J. Toswell Western University, London, Ontario
Typesetting and IT	David DeAngelis First Circle Publishing, London, Ontario
Junior Editor	Emily Pickard Western University, London, Ontario

ROMARD wishes to thank Western University for its support through the Scholarly Journals at Western program.

ROMARD (ISSN 0098-647X) is published annually at Western University (London, Ontario). Inquiries concerning publication should be submitted to the Chief Editor at romard@romard.org.

The current annual rate is $25 USD plus shipping for individuals. For all subscription inquiries, including institutional subscriptions and back issue orders, please contact subscriber-inquiries@romard.org. ROMARD may also be purchased online at www.romard.org and on www.amazon.com.

Contents

	Introduction **Charlotte Steenbrugge &** **Alexandra F. Johnston**	1
I	The Thaïs Scenario: Public Women, Penance, and Performance **Marla Carlson**	7
	"Since I have your good leave to go away": Negotiating desire in *The Merchant of Venice* **Erin Weinberg**	25
	"Most excellent warriers, very valiaunt": Reading Amazons in *A Midsummer Night's* *Dream* and *The Two Noble Kinsmen* **Kirsten Inglis**	41
	"Are You My Sweet Heart?": *Bonduca* and the Failure of Chivalric Masculinity **Andrew Bretz**	59
	Mucedorus, Shakespeare, and the Persistence of Romance **Dimitry Senyshyn**	73
	"The Actors of the Playe were Countreymen": the disastrous performance of *Mucedorus* in 1653 **Alexandra F. Johnston**	85

II	*La farce du Poulier à six personnages* (The Farce of the Chicken Coop for Six Characters) BnF Ms fr. 24341 (ff. 132ᵛ–144ᵛ) **Mario Longtin and Richard J. Moll**	**99**
	La farce du Poulier à six personnages (in modern French spelling)	**109**
	The Farce of the Chicken Coop for Six Characters (adapted into English verse)	**141**

Contributor Biographies — **171**

Introduction
Charlotte Steenbrugge & Alexandra F. Johnston

In November 2013, *Poculi Ludique Societas* organised a conference to shed greater light on *Mucedorus*, a late sixteenth-century English romance play that was once hugely popular but is now largely overlooked. And in April 2014, it held another symposium at the University of Toronto to accompany the production of two Middle Dutch plays, namely *Vanden Winter ende vanden Somer* (*Of Winter and Summer*) and *Lanseloet van Denemerken* (*Lancelot of Denmark*). Despite the differences in language, locality, and time of these three works (the Dutch plays probably stem from the fourteenth century), and indeed in their content and style, it quickly became evident that they have a great deal in common and that many of the presentations of two such dissimilar symposia would combine beautifully to make a significant contribution to our understanding of the use of romance as a genre and of love as a theme in medieval and early modern drama. Most of the contributions to this volume derive from papers at these two symposia, and others were invited in order to present a more rounded volume.

Because of the nature of the surviving texts, it is easy to assume that European medieval drama consisted almost exclusively of serious, religious plays – such as morality, miracle, biblical, and saints' plays. However, particularly in the northern tradition, evidence suggests a lively tradition of secular plays, both comic and serious, going back to the earliest records. For example, there is Adam de la Halle's comical-pastoral *Jeu de Robin et Marion* (*Play of Robin and Marion*) from the 1280s, in which Marion resists the amorous advances of a knight in order to stay faithful to her sweetheart Robin, and *La fuite des enfans Aymery de Narbonne* (*The Flight of the children of Aymeri of Narbonne*) was performed in the market square of Lille in 1351; the latter was presumably closely related in terms of content to one or several of the *chansons de geste* concerning Guillaume d'Orange.[1] In German-speaking areas there was a long-standing tradition of comic Shrovetide plays of *Fastnachtspiele* that satirized the follies of mankind represented by shrewish or bickering housewives, village simpletons, lecherous priests, and unfaithful husbands that culminated in the work of Hans Sachs of Nuremberg (1494-1576) who published eighty-five such short farces. In the Low Countries, one of the earliest references to a play dates from 1373 Oudenaarde and mentions a fight "twelke al gheviel int Spel van Strasengijs" ("which all happened in the play of Trazegnies"); the play presumably presented more or less the same story as has come down to us in the French romance *L'Histoire de Gillion de Trazegnies*.[2] This play, or a play with similar subject matter, was also performed in Dendermonde in 1447 and formed part of the library of a Ghent guild in 1532, arguing both for the longevity of its popularity and its considerable geographical spread.[3] Other references to romance plays likewise mention recognizable romance or *chanson de geste* stories, such as a play "van Amys ende van Amelis" ("of Amis and Amiloun," Bruges, 1412-13), "van der batailge van Roelande ende Oliviere" ("of the battle of Roland and Oliver," Geraardsbergen, 1423), "van Tristram" ("of Tristan," Venlo, 1459), and "van Florijsse ende Blanchefloere" ("of Floris and Blancheflour," Tielt, 1483).[4]

Indeed the earliest plays to survive in Middle Dutch are nearly all secular and all about love: several farces that present typical *fabliau* stories of adultery and overbearing wives, one debate play *Vanden Winter ende vanden Somer* (*Of Winter and Summer*) about which is the best season in which to love, and three romance plays (*Gloriant*, *Esmoreit*, and *Lanseloet van Denemerken* (*Lancelot of Denmark*)).[5] These plays all survive in the Van Hulthem manuscript, which is dated c.1410, but the texts are clearly not originals and the plays themselves may therefore be considerably older.[6] The romance plays may well have had an extended performance history and long-lasting popularity. *Lancelot of Denmark*, for instance, may have been performed from the fourteenth to the eighteenth century. It is not simply one of the oldest surviving Middle Dutch plays in manuscript context, it is also the earliest surviving printed play from the Low Countries.[7] There is evidence to suggest that this play may have been performed in Diest in 1412 (which is more or less contemporaneous with the Van Hulthem manuscript) and it was put on in Zwolle in 1549 and 1550.[8] We even have two actor's rolls for *Lancelot of Denmark*, which belonged to a rhetoricians' chamber in 's Gravenpolder and "dese rolle gespeelt opt jaer 1720" ("this role was played in the year 1720") is written on the back of one of these documents.[9]

On the other hand, while many of these plays may have been what we would label "secular," a hard and fast distinction between religious and secular (and, indeed, between serious and comic) is difficult to maintain with regard to at least some of these plays. We do not know whether the Bruges play of Amis and Amiloun (1412-13) featured the miraculous intervention of the Virgin Mary, as does the dramatic version in the fourteenth-century *Miracles de Notre Dame*, but that must certainly remain a possibility. The play about the "coninc van Argon" ("king of Aragon") which was performed in Antwerp in 1495 was in all probability related to the *Miracles de Notre Dame* story of Thierry of Aragon which presents a romance story, but one clothed in a marked layer of religious sentiment.[10] (That confluence of secular and religious elements is, of course, also not uncommon for non-dramatic romances, such as *Robert of Cisyle*, of which more below.) Likewise, in Tielt in 1438 a play was performed which seems to have been a romance play, but which strongly recalls saints' lives as well: payment is made for the city officials "omme de Bekeeringe te zien spelene van den Ruddere, twelke een goed exempel was" ("to see the conversion of the knight played, which was a good example").[11]

One of the distinctive characteristics of medieval literature is the way in which conventions from one genre spill over into others with absolutely no regard for the sacred or the secular. This fluidity applies to northern drama too, as can be seen in some of the examples above or the sheep stealing farce in the Towneley *Second Shepherds' Play*. Joanne Findon has pointed out the clever use of romance elements in Digby *Mary Magdalen*, a late medieval English saint's play.[12] In the 1492 *Mystère de sainte Barbe en cinq journées* (The Mystery of St Barbara in Five Days) there is the farcical interlude with Maliverné, Linar, and Maunoury. And the devils from the *Mystère de saint Martin de Seurre* (The Mystery of St Martin of Seurre) (1496) appear in the accompanying farce, *La farce du meunier qui donne son âme au diable* (The Farce of the Miller who Gives his Soul to the Devil). This permeability of genre is also to be detected in early modern plays – *Mucedorus*, for instance, is very self-conscious about its mongrel generic status – despite a rise of genre purists like Sir Philip Sidney who lamented "how all their plays be neither right tragedies, nor right comedies, mingling kings and clowns … with neither decency nor discretion, so as neither admiration and commiseration, nor the right sportfulness, is by their mongrel tragi-comedy obtained."[13] It is presumably to a large extent this flexibility which allowed playwrights both to address serious issues through fanciful stories and to offer light-hearted escapism that can explain the enduring and widespread popularity of plays of love and romance in medieval and early modern Europe.

In England information concerning serious and/or comic plays about love is rather more scarce, but there are some early references to romance plays here too. Mantingh has argued that one of the reasons why there are few references to romance plays in the Low Countries is that they appear to have been predominantly performed by professional companies, which tend not to rely on civic or ecclesiastical subsidies.[14] The same could well be the case for England too. Moreover, even when such acting troupes did receive some subsidy, the nature of the play performed was probably of no great interest to the accountant and thus unlikely to be recorded; chances are that recurrent, well-known, local plays were more likely to be named in the records. But the exhaustive research collected in the Records of Early English Drama volumes does show that there were some such romance plays. In Coventry, there appears to have been a Hock Tuesday tradition involving a play celebrating the defeat of the Danes (apparently women had greatly contributed to this defeat). It was performed, though intermittently, from at least 1416 until 1576; it was also presented before Elizabeth I at Kenilworth in 1575.[15] In a letter that mentions this Kenilworth performance, the presenter figure, Captain Cox, is explicitly linked with romances:

> great ouersight hath he in matters of storie: For az for king Arthurz book, Huon of Burdeaus, The foour suns of Aymon, Beuys of Hampton, The squyre of lo degree, The knight of courtesy, and the Lady Faguell, Frederik of Gene, Syr Eglamoour, Sir Tryamoour, Syr Lamwell, Syr Isenbras, Syr Gawyn, Olyuer of the Castl … with many moe then I rehearz heere: I beleeue hee haue them all at hiz fingers endz.[16]

Given that Captain Cox only appears in connection to the play, this emphatic mention of his knowledge of romances seems to imply that the content or performance of the play was in some way akin to romance literature. In September 1424 local players performed a play of "Amys and Amylon" for Prior Richard Parentyn at Bicester Priory; considering the size of the payment, Alexandra F. Johnston has argued that this play featured elaborate staging, which makes heavenly intervention by the Virgin, similar to that seen in the French miracle play, quite likely.[17] A "ludus de kynge Robert of Cesill" was also performed in Lincoln in 1452-53 and we have references to plays on Robert of Sicily being performed in Chester in 1529-30.[18] Presumably the story of these plays reflected that of the surviving romance *Robert of Cisyle*, which is awash with moral and religious sentiment; it is therefore likely that the plays also contained these more religious notes. The spread of the Robert of Sicily plays in geographical and chronological terms, and the long performance history of the Coventry play also argue for a vibrant tradition of romance plays. Unfortunately, none of these medieval examples has survived. Admittedly, there are many more references to, and indeed texts of, such plays from sixteenth- and seventeenth-century England. But rather than assuming that romance plays and plays with romance themes were a new development in the sixteenth century, it seems wiser, in view of the evidence from the continent and the few fifteenth-century English references, and indeed in view of romance elements in plays such as the Digby *Mary Magdalen*, to think of romance plays as a popular genre from early on. We do, moreover, have two early medieval English semi-dramatic *fabliaux*, which present traditional stories of love, or at least of lust, in *Dame Sirith* (c.1275) and *Interludium de clerico et puella* (c.1300).

The essays in section one of this volume are concerned with the northern tradition and attest to the popularity, and indeed the usefulness, of the theme of love and the romance genre for medieval and early modern drama, as it was used to scrutinize and address any number of issues, especially those related to gender. As Carlson shows, Hrotsvit's *The Conversion of the Harlot Thaïs* uses a traditional Terentian story not so much to highlight the contrast between sexual lust and the chaste love of God (although it does that too), as to betray anxiety about the conflict between the political role of powerful Ottonian women and their religious vocation of withdrawal from the world. Such a withdrawal from the world, and consequent lack of power, is what Portia is subjected to and objects to in *The Merchant of Venice*, and here Bassanio's quest for her hand in marriage and, as Weinberg cogently argues, his romantic relationship with Antonio finally allow her to pursue some of that intellectual freedom she desires. Both Bretz and Inglis demonstrate how seventeenth-century playwrights use romance conventions to voice concerns about masculinity and femininity. But whereas Fletcher seems to undermine the traditional romance view of masculinity through his portrayal of both the victim and the perpetrator of rape (Bretz), Shakespeare and Fletcher's portrayal of Hippolyta and Emilia endorses the silencing of women which the genre often entails (Inglis). While plays about love and romance plays could thus be used to scrutinize important issues, they could also offer light-hearted entertainment. Senyshyn places Shakespeare's later plays in the context of the popularity and innocuous nature but also the self-conscious theatricality of romance plays such as *Mucedorus*. And Johnston demonstrates that the appeal of *Mucedorus* was neither confined to London nor ceased with the closing of the playhouses in 1642, and thus makes a potent case for the continuing tradition of dramatic performance of romance plays well into the seventeenth century in England.

The contributions to this volume all demonstrate the significance of romance, both as a genre and a theme, for medieval and early modern drama and will hopefully stimulate greater interest in this multifaceted area of research. We have also included in section two an edition and verse translation of an early modern French farce (Longtin and Moll) in the hope that this will encourage scholars, students, and theatre practitioners to stage these fascinating, and as the *Poculi Ludique Societas* productions showed, eminently performable plays.

We would like to thank all the contributors to this volume for their diligence and enthusiasm, in particular David Klausner, Mario Longtin, MJ Toswell, David DeAngelis, and Emily Pickard.

Notes

1. J. te Winkel, *De ontwikkelingsgang der Nederlandsche letterkunde. Deel 2: Geschiedenis der Nederlansche letterkunde van Middeleeuwen en Rederijkerstijd* (Haarlem: De Erven F. Bohn, 1922), p. 156.
2. Erwin Mantingh, "'... twelke al gheviel int Spel van Strasengijs'. Naar aanleiding van een ongekend drama in Oudenaarde anno 1371," *Queeste* 7 (2000): 38-50.
3. Mantingh, "... twelke al gheviel," p. 43.
4. Dieuwke E. van der Poel, "De voorstelling is voorbij: Vermeldingen van wereldlijk toneel en de casus van *Strasengijs*," in *Spel en Spektakel: Middeleeuws toneel in de Lage Landen*, ed. by Hans van Dijk, Bart Ramakers, e.a. (Amsterdam: Prometheus, 2001), pp. 111-132 at 115-118.
5. Two of the farces deal with more religious matters. *Die Hexe* (*The Witch*) is about a suspected case of witchcraft and the fragmentary *Truwanten* (*Tramps*) presents a criticism of people of dubious religious standing begging for a living.
6. Hans van Dijk, "The Drama Texts in the Van Hulthem Manuscript," in *Medieval Dutch Literature in its European Context*, ed. E. Kooper (Cambridge: Cambridge University Press, 1994), pp. 283-296 at 286-288.
7. Dirk Coigneau, "Drama in druk, tot circa 1540," in *Spel en Spektakel: Middeleeuws toneel in de Lage Landen*, ed. Hans van Dijk, Bart Ramakers, e.a. (Amsterdam: Prometheus, 2001), pp. 201-214 at p. 201.
8. Van der Poel, "De voorstelling," p. 116.
9. http://www.literatuurgeschiedenis.nl/lg/middeleeuwen/tekst/lgme006.html.
10. Van der Poel, "De voorstelling," p. 119.
11. Van der Poel, "De voorstelling," p. 117.
12. Joanne Findon, "Napping in the Arbour in the Digby *Mary Magdalen* Play," *Early Theatre* 9 (2006): 35-55.
13. Sir Philip Sidney, *The Defense of Poesy*, ed. Lewis Soen (Lincoln, Nebraska: University of Nebraska Press, 1970), 49.
14. Mantingh, "... twelke al gheviel," p. 48.
15. R.W. Ingram, ed., *Records of Early English Drama: Coventry* (Toronto: University of Toronto Press, 1981), xx.
16. Ingram, *Records*, p. 273.
17. Alexandra F. Johnston, "'Amys and Amylon' at Bicester Priory," *REED Newsletter* 28 (1993): 15-18 at 16-17.
18. James Stokes, ed., *Records of Early English Drama: Lincolnshire* (Toronto: University of Toronto Press, 2009), 115, and Elizabeth Baldwin, Lawrence M. Clopper, and David Mills, eds, *Records of Early English Drama: Cheshire (including Chester)* (Toronto: University of Toronto Press, 2007), 70.

The Thaïs Scenario: Public Women, Penance, and Performance
Marla Carlson

*I*n what sense might one consider Hrotsvit of Gandersheim's *The Conversion of the Harlot Thaïs* (c.970) to present love on the early medieval stage? In the preface to her six dramas, the tenth-century canoness explains that she set out to praise "the laudable chastity of sacred virgins" as a substitute for "the shameless acts of lascivious women" in Terence's six comedies.[1] A chaste love of God motivates her Christian heroes and heroines, who seek not the marriage that typically resolves a comedy's plot but rather a return to God in death with the promise of resurrection. Where her Terentian models use a young man's love to motivate a clever slave's machinations on his behalf, the holy actions of Hrotsvit's Christians oppose the lust of pagans. In her two harlot redemption plays, a hermit poses as a lover in order to bring a woman back from prostitution to blessed chastity. Regula Meyer Evitt has read these plays in the context of tenth-century incest. She focuses primarily upon *The Fall and Repentance of Mary* (also known as *Abraham*) and proposes that the hermit Abraham was in fact the lover disguised as a monk who seduced the girl while she was under his care, precipitating her fall into harlotry. His disguise as lover thus inverts the earlier disguise and rights the wrong.[2]

Although carnal motivation makes these characters easier for a modern audience to comprehend and the action more familiar and lively, I would assert the value of analyzing them in all their tenth-century strangeness. The first part of my argument analyzes the non-Aristotelian structure of Hrotsvit's *Thaïs* play in order to make sense of the characters and their actions. I wish to avoid treating these dramatic figures as actual persons and will not explore their psychological motivations or personal histories outside what the dramatic text explicitly presents. Hrotsvit wrote these plays nearly a full millennium before psychological realism began to encourage such speculation. Her texts provide our only evidence for tenth-century dramatic convention, and they offer nothing to suggest that the characters' words and actions conceal hidden depths: as the hermit Pafnutius puts it in the play's opening exchange with his disciples, "The man whose heart is grieved shows in his countenance, too, that he is grieved" (93).[3] Although he adopts a disguise in order to approach Thaïs, the device is fully transparent to the audience. Yet Hrotsvit did not write in a vacuum, and the relation between her plays and the lived experience of tenth-century Saxons bears investigation. Evitt offers a convincing argument for the *Mary* play as evidence of Ottonian anxieties about nonconsensual sexual relations as well as marriages that might be either too closely consanguineous or politically inconvenient.[4] I agree with her that the lives of the women who participated in ruling the Ottonian empire and populated its religious foundations are key to understanding the plays. Hrotsvit lived among them, and they were almost certainly among the audience for whatever presentation the plays may have been given – whether or not that included anything that we would recognize as theatrical. Although the figure of the harlot suggests a focus on sexual desire and lust, my analysis of the *Thaïs* play shifts that focus to the role of women in the political sphere, to money and power.

The second portion of my argument analyzes the scenario of containment, repeatedly activated when public women disrupt social equilibrium. "Public woman" is an outmoded euphemism for sex worker, of course, and I use it here to signal the continuum between prostitution and other disruptions of social harmony by women who must then be put in their place to restore the status quo. Hrotsvit's play presents the harlot Thaïs as a disruption of harmony, both macro- and microcosmic, but also presents her body as container for a soul, already potentially harmonic. The hermit Pafnutius encloses the harlot's body within an anchoritic cell, a more secure container, in order to restore harmony at all levels. The specific conception of "scenario" with which I'm working comes from Diana Taylor's *The Archive and the Repertoire*. Hrotsvit's writings as well as the chronicles by her contemporaries such as Thietmar of Merseburg and Widukind of Corvey belong to the *archive* of Ottonian culture; that is, the repository of its material remains and especially its textual traces. Taylor argues for the value of also paying close attention to the "so-called ephemeral *repertoire* of embodied practice/knowledge" through which culture is transmitted from person to living person. Often these practices congeal as a *scenario* that we find reactivated in multiple times and places, even continuing to structure present-day encounters.[5] Consider the scenario of a woman endangered by her very presence in public space, which has resurfaced in internationally reported cases of rape in India since 2012; or the scenario of a woman endangered by her performance of masculine-coded behaviors such as drinking, which features in the contemporary dialogue on college campuses about sexual consent.[6] These endangerment scenarios connect loosely to the scenario of containment that structures programs to rehabilitate sex workers by getting them off the streets and into residential treatment and training programs.[7] An awareness of such scenarios can alert the scholar to traces in the historical archive of a significant embodied repertoire that might be easily overlooked.

Hrotsvit's *Thaïs* play activates a specifically medieval scenario of containment featuring enclosure to restore the harmony that a public woman has disrupted. Through enclosure, the woman's body becomes overwhelmingly present for her but absent from the public world, and her material circumstances are brought into conformity with her befouled soul. I will argue that the scenario of containment, visible not only in the Christian legend of Thaïs and in Terence's *Eunuchus* but also – without the prostitution – in the archival traces of the anchoritic repertoire, helps to elucidate the connections between Hrotsvit's *Thaïs* play and the disruption brought about by the youthful escapes of powerful aristocratic women from abbeys such as Gandersheim. Like Hrotsvit's dramas, these chronicles, *vitae*, and anchoritic guidebooks are literary works that use the tropes available within the genre but, as Anneke B. Mulder-Bakker observes with respect to the guidebooks, they may not fully reflect historical events and practices.[8] In other words, the archival traces are not fully adequate to the repertoire of embodied practices, but the shape of the reiterated scenario reveals something about the place at which they meet.

Containing Thaïs

In keeping with Evitt's suspicions about Abraham, modern treatments of the Thaïs scenario have indeed featured a hermit tempted by lust for the whore whom he sets out to redeem. The most prominent is Anatole France's novel, *Thaïs*, which was first published in 1890 and formed the basis of Massenet's opera and some largely forgotten plays.[9] The novel's Paphnuce, who came from the aristocracy, had prefaced his life of Christian austerity with a dissolute youth in Alexandria, in the course of which he had first encountered the actress Thaïs. In his desert hermitage he finds himself haunted by the memory and sets off to save her. Thaïs had traveled in the opposite direction, from Christian poverty to corrupt wealth. As a child, she was baptized through the influence of a Nubian slave. After Paphnuce converts Thaïs, both characters reverse their trajectory. Thaïs repents, returns to her Christian belief, and ends up a holy woman due to the severity of her penance. Paphnuce finally realizes that he has loved Thaïs all along, throws off holiness, and rushes to her, too late. Hrotsvit's play shows no interest in this sort of romantic love, nor in the action, reversals, and recognition that characterize the novel's plot, which conforms to expectations of dramatic structure shaped by the neo-Aristotelian concepts that dominated eurocentric criticism from the Renaissance until the late twentieth century. Aristotle holds that plot is the most important element of tragedy; that the action of a play determines the characters to be included, not vice versa; and that two components of the plot, reversal and recognition, are the "most important things with which a tragedy enthralls" its audience.[10] Even today, many playwriting teachers assert that a drama must be based on action, which is best developed through conflict between characters. According to this line of thinking, a good dramatization of the Thaïs story should *show* the harlot's lascivious behavior and her corruption of men rather than telling about it; Pafnutius should convert her only after a struggle; and if her enclosure and penance are to feature prominently, then she should be shown encountering some obstacle while enclosed in the anchoritic cell, which Pafnutius could help her to overcome, resulting in her good death. At the very least, she should struggle with herself.

Hrotsvit, of course, wrote prior to the European rediscovery of Aristotle's *Poetics*. She had Terence as a model and very likely had access to commentaries on Terence by the fourth-century grammarians Evanthius (*De Fabula*) and Donatus (*De Comoedia*).[11] Although other characters in the play describe Thaïs as lascivious, any lascivious behavior would have to be interpolated by a performer: the dialogue contains no such implied stage directions. Furthermore, there is almost no conflict between characters in the *Thaïs* play. Her lovers object when Thaïs burns her wealth, and she is initially reluctant to be enclosed in a cell that she must befoul with her bodily waste. But neither of these conflicts really drives the play; instead, the action develops as a working out of the problem introduced in Pafnutius' opening conversation with his disciples. As anyone who has used this play in a theatre class will likely be aware, readers often skim what they perceive to be a tedious, pedantic scene. Dr. Mary Kay Gamel's 2003 production at the University of California at Santa Cruz staged this scene in a comic register, a reasonable strategy for bringing it to a modern audience; that is, playing Pafnutius as a ridiculous pedant and his students' questions as mockery. This interpretation has satisfied my students,[12] but it does not satisfy me. Instead, a structural analysis based on Evanthius and Donatus has led me independently to David Chamberlain's conclusion that "the action of *Conversio Thaidis* is a brilliant embodiment of the ideas about music developed in [the play's first scene]."[13]

Both grammarians describe a four-part structure for comedy, beginning with a prologue, which they identify as the only occasion for extrinsic address to the audience. Hrotsvit would likely have been familiar with Terence's prologues but begins her dramas directly with dialogue between characters.[14] During the first section of a play, the *protasis*, Donatus says that "part of the story is explained, part held back to arouse suspense among the audience."[15] In this *protasis*, Hrotsvit explains the discord in the human world of which Thaïs is the proximate cause and which Pafnutius will resolve. Thus Pafnutius' conversation with his disciples presents the play's problem, and does so through an explication of Boethian philosophy. In response to his disciples' query about the cloudy countenance that displays his grief, Pafnutius explains that God is injured by human dissonance (95) – as Chamberlain points out, explicitly characterizing this as a metaphor and thus preparing Hrotsvit's audience to map one realm onto another.[16] The explanation begins with the correspondence of microcosm (man) to macrocosm, each comprising four contrary elements that God makes concordant "according to the regular arrangements of harmony." The microcosm, though, has components "much more contrary than those four" material elements: the body is material and mortal; the soul, immaterial and immortal. Even so, the body and the soul can be harmonized because "nothing is contrary to the essential substance, which contains within itself all contraries" (96). To explain this harmonization, Pafnutius turns to music, a branch of the philosophical *quadrivium* (together with arithmetic, geometry, and astronomy).

The discussion of music not only establishes the necessity for harmonizing material body and immaterial soul but also positions dissimilarity as a precondition for harmony. As Chamberlain explains, "when things are either perfectly similar or when they are so different in nature that they are joined by 'nulla ratio proportionis,' then no concord can be created. Without dissimilarity, there cannot be concord. Discord is the raw material of music in the play."[17] Pafnutius goes into considerable detail about the arithmetical relationships that characterize all three kinds of music, celestial, human, and instrumental; for example, musical instruments can make "the same number of intervals, the same lengths, and the same agreement of sounds" as the planets make in relation to one another (98), and Pafnutius offers speculative explanations for the fact that humans are unable to hear the music of the spheres (99). The disciples then turn the conversation to human music, which Pafnutius locates

> Not only, as I said before, in the union of body and soul, and not only in the emission of high and low sounds, but also in the pulse of our veins and in the measures of our limbs, as in the parts of our fingers, where we find the same mathematical proportions of measure as we mentioned in harmonies, because music is not only the agreement of sounds but also that of dissimilar entities. (100)

After an exchange about the difficulty of understanding this musical philosophy that one might interpret as the author's characteristic apology for presumption,[18] the conversation moves to the cause of Pafnutius' grief: the beautiful whore Thaïs disrupts the harmony of the human sphere as men fight for her favors, spend all of their money on her, and – not least – damn themselves by indulging their lust (102-3). The *protasis* ends with the "happy idea" that will resolve the problem: Pafnutius will "visit her, disguised as a lover, to see if perchance she might be recovered from her worthless and frivolous life" (103). In musical terms, he will enter into the dissonance and harmonize its discordant elements, thereby restoring harmony throughout the microcosm and, by correspondence, the macrocosm. The precise method of harmonization is "held back to arouse suspense among the audience," as Donatus puts it.

The holy man's journey to Thaïs begins the play's *epitasis,* and his return to his disciples ends it. Evanthius defines this section as "the knot of all the error"; Donatus, as a "complication of the story, by excellence of which its elements are intertwined."[19] A group of Thaïs's lovers guides Pafnutius to her. They embody the discord that she produces, and Pafnutius pretends to be similarly disordered. Once in her presence, though, he need take no active part in converting Thaïs aside from abandoning his false countenance and weeping in grief: Christian faith already exists deep within the harlot and has only to be uncovered – discord itself seeks harmony. Hrotsvit does not include the sort of circumstantial explanation that Anatole France thought necessary, such as a Christian upbringing before Thaïs became a whore, and Thaïs herself introduces the theme of an enclosure that simultaneously discloses: Pafnutius asks her for a private room, hidden away, and Thaïs acknowledges one "so hidden, so secret that no one besides me knows it, except for God" (106) – that is, the heart in which God is already present. Having acknowledged the inner part of herself so dissimilar from her outward sins, Thaïs weeps with Pafnutius and readily accepts his instruction to withdraw from the world but knows that she must first burn her "ill-gotten and depraved" wealth (108). Over the course of this scene, he has brought her outward countenance into harmony with her grievous spiritual state;[20] now, destroying the outward sign of that which must be eliminated within, Thaïs burns her goods and abandons her distraught lovers.

To achieve harmony, Thaïs will enter an anchoritic cell – a container more secure than her own overly exposed body. Jocelyn Wogan-Brown notes that the thirteenth-century *Ancrene Wisse* "structur[es] the anchoress's physical and spiritual existence as a series of enclosures: her cell and her body enclosing her heart and her soul, her heart 'God's chamber.'"[21] Pafnutius restates the play's central problem and explains why enclosure is the proper remedy: "the sickness of both body and soul must be cured by the medicine of contraries" (113). The anchoritic cell brings these contrary elements together to create harmony in human music, just as instrumental music brings together high and low tones. Thaïs's embarrassment and disgust at the thought that she must "perform all necessary functions of the body in the very same room," which will "soon be uninhabitable because of the stench" (115), leads to an extended discussion of the bad smell as appropriate expiation for "the evil sweetness of alluring delight." To her concern that "there is not one spot left, dignified and pure, where [Thaïs] could invoke the name of God's majesty," Pafnutius replies that she is not to speak God's name, but to cry and be humiliated: "Clearly you should pray not with words but with tears; not with your tinkling voice's melodious art but with the bursting of your penitent heart" (115). In notably similar terms, the second part of the *Ancrene Wisse*, "about the custody of the heart through the five senses," refigures the sensory universe of the anchoress around speech, with a passing metaphorical reference to smell:

> The devil of hell with his army passes straight through the mouth that is always open into the heart ... Often when we start talking, we mean to say a few well-chosen words; but the tongue is slippery because it wades in water, and glides on easily from a few words into many ... [speech] grows from a drop into a great flood which drowns the soul; for with the flow of speech the heart flows away, so that it cannot be properly collected together for a long time afterwards ... And the nearer our mouth is to the world, the farther it is from God; and the more it is polluted in speech, the less it is heard in prayer.... That is why often we call on him but he turns away from our voice and will not listen to it, because all it does is stink to him of all the world's chatter and babble.[22]

Like the *Ancrene Wisse*'s references to the organs of speech, presented with liquid and watery images, Thaïs's discussion of bodily functions and bad smells foregrounds the body's materiality, and Pafnutius's injunction to pray through tears rather than words guides her instead toward the immaterial soul. Thaïs sees the logic at once: she is filthy, and the cell will become filthy. Once this harmony has been achieved, she can begin the spiritual journey to freedom from materiality – which can come only with death. Thaïs's enclosure will manifest the harmony that was always present – as potential – within her. Completing the play's *epitasis*, Pafnutius withdraws again from the profane world.

Hrotsvit stages none of Thaïs's penance and transformation, which she has described in advance through dialogue between Pafnutius and Thaïs. She now redescribes it from a distance, by means of prayer and a vision within the play's *catastrophe* – for Donatus, the unraveling of the intertwined elements; for Evanthius, the resolution, happy ending, and recognition of past events such that everyone understands what has happened and accepts it.[23] After three years have passed, Pafnutius consults another hermit, Antonius, to discover through communal prayer whether the penance succeeded. Antonius's disciple Paul has a vision – which he initially misinterprets – revealing that it has. Pafnutius then visits Thaïs and rejoices with her as she prepares to die. This final encounter requires no journey because both microcosm and macrocosm correspond in harmony, and the final scene reinforces and clarifies the play's resolution rather than providing further plot development.

Containing Early Medieval Women

Anchoritic enclosure contrasts sharply with the relative freedom enjoyed by aristocratic Ottonian women – including those at Gandersheim. Hrotsvit did not dramatize her own experience or that of her companions. Terence's *Eunuchus* offered a *meretrix* named Thaïs, and the *vita* of Saint Thaïs provided details of her conversion and penance. Beyond these literary sources, Hrotsvit would likely have known of at least two female anchorites, Liutbirg of Wendhausen (d.870) and Wiborada of St. Gall (d.926).[24] Because Liutbirg's exemplary life of service to others was not enough to satisfy her intense need for penance nor were the severe fasts and all-night vigils that endangered her health, she sought and received episcopal approval to finish her life in a tiny cell. Her *vita* indicates that she spent most of her time praying, but that she also "instructed the women who came to her" and engaged in the "many arts of women" at which she was skilled – for example, she kept "a small charcoal fire in her cell for dyes of different colors."[25] Liutbirg's biographer narrates many trials that she underwent during her thirty years of enclosure, including a demon who caused her cell to be completely overrun with mice.[26] Wiborada, the patron saint of libraries and the first woman to be canonized (in 1047 by Pope Clement II), also withdrew to her anchorhold after an exemplary Christian life, which included caring for the patients that her brother Hitto brought to her.[27] After their joint pilgrimage to Rome, Wiborada convinced Hitto to enter the monastery at St. Gall, and she returned to their estate for a life of fasting and prayer. A second *vita* written around 1062 includes traces of discord in this barely public sphere: gossip began to circulate that she was staying up all night to engage in practices less wholesome than prayer, as did rumors of incest with her brother. Bishop Salamon of Constance summoned her to trial by ordeal in order to end these rumors, and she was indeed exonerated. Even so, she subsequently chose to spend the rest of her life in a tiny cell attached to the church that her brother served.[28] She worked as a bookbinder for the library at St. Gall and foresaw a Hungarian invasion in 926 in time to warn the monks, enabling them to save the books and wine. The invaders burned the church and killed Wiborada with their axes.[29] Wiborada's cell also held Rechild (d. 947), whom Wiborada had nursed back to health and who survived her. Another female recluse, Kerhild, lived there from 952-1008. The cell at this monastery's older church, St. George, housed the widow Bertrada from 959-980 and then for thirty years the monk Hartker (d. 1011 or 1017), and the nun Kotelinde was also enclosed at St. Gall during this period. The nun Caritas entered a cell at the monastery in Worms some time before 1025, and Thietmar of Merseberg compared the recluse Sisu (d. 1018), enclosed at Drübeck in Saxony for 64 years, to the desert fathers because she allowed her body to be eaten by maggots as had St. Simeon Stylites atop his pillar.[30] The practice of enclosure was spreading among ascetic monks and nuns in Hrotsvit's part of the world during the tenth century. During the eleventh, anchoritism became even more popular and by the end of that century the practice also shifted to the laity.

In spite of all their contrasts, Hrotsvit's harlot-conversion dramas, early medieval anchoritic practices, and the aristocratic Ottonian woman's enclosure in a monastery all activate the scenario of containment. The walls that enclosed Hrotsvit at Gandersheim were quite porous, and I have come to think that her plays urged a more stringent separation from the world. She invariably presents segregation of the sexes as the most desirable arrangement. As already discussed, the public sphere is a space of degradation for the harlots Mary and Thaïs, and their hermit rescuers enter this space only in order to enclose the women in an anchorhold. Across the other four plays, lustful pagan men present a danger to Christian women who are either virgins or living in chaste marriage. *The Martyrdom of the Holy Virgins Fides, Spes, and Karitas* (also known as *Sapientia*) opens with the breach wrought by Christian women in pagan Rome: wives are alienated and will no longer eat or sleep with men (126). Try as they might, men have no power over women in Hrotsvit's gender-segregated dramatic world, except in cases where a spiritual superior such as Abraham or Pafnutius offers advice that a woman voluntarily accepts.[31] I propose that the dramas and the historical record bear the traces of Ottonian discord surrounding women, wealth, and power. The scenario of containment configures the efforts at harmonization in sexual terms.

Others have summarized the relevant history, but it bears repeating here.[32] During the tenth century, the Liudolfing dynasty brought together the eastern portions of a Europe that had been fragmented since the end of the Carolingian empire, ended the Magyar invasions, and conquered Slavic lands further east. Beginning with Liudolf of Saxony (d. 866) and continuing through his successors Henry I (duke of the Saxons from 866, king of the Saxons and Franks from 919), Otto I (king of the Saxons and Franks from 936, Holy Roman emperor from 962, d. 973), Otto II (co-emperor from 967), Otto III (from 983), and Henry II (from 1002), marriage and religious foundations served as crucial tools for consolidating power – provided the women married as they were required to and handled the income of their monasteries in such a way as to advance the interests of the empire. Each of these rulers designated a single successor and arranged ecclesiastical careers for other sons, who became crucial to administering the empire. A daughter would be educated in a religious house from around the age of five until she was either brought out for marriage to create a political alliance or made abbess. Later, the women of the ruling family returned to a religious house as widows, often to one where a daughter was abbess.[33]

Gandersheim, founded in 852 by Liudolf of Saxony and his wife Oda, remained especially close to the family. Their daughter Hathumoda was its first abbess. When the canonesses had portentous nightmares that the abbey would collapse once she was gone, Hathumoda appealed to Louis the Younger, husband of her sister Liutgard and king of the Franks. He gave it royal status in 877, placed it under the supervision of the bishop of Hildesheim, and increased its endowment. His successor contributed more vineyards.[34] Hathumoda's sisters Gerberga I and Christina succeeded her as abbess in turn. Oda lived there with her daughters after Liudolf's death in 866 and pressured her grandchildren to bestow gifts upon Gandersheim, and her property passed to the abbey when she died in 912. Property, as well as other rights and duties, could be derived through matrilineal as well as patrilineal inheritance. Although a woman's husband had control over her hereditary property, he did not own it, and if she outlived him – which she quite likely would – she might well end up with more land than her husband had possessed and could then protect her estate by founding a religious house. At least 36 such foundations for women were established between 919 and 1024, more than the number of male monasteries created during this period, and they were concentrated in secure regions rather than in border lands.[35] The Liudolfing women exercised primary control of these monastic properties. The empress was often lay abbess of a foundation and controlled its money, except for the portion established as the mense to support the canonesses. These women, such as Hrotsvit, were similarly placed in religious houses to suit the dynastic purposes of their aristocratic families and could be retrieved to make marriages or left in place to take vows (or not).

Henry the Fowler succeeded his grandfather as duke of the Saxons and was also elected king of the Franks in 919. He had a son, Thangmar, by a nun or canoness named Hatheburg, whom he restored to her convent in order to marry Mathilda, a student in the convent at Herford whose abbess arranged this marriage and chaperoned the courtship. Henry designated their son Otto as his sole successor in 929 and arranged a marriage to Edith, the daughter of an English king.[36] To avoid dividing the kingdom among his children, Henry had arranged an ecclesiastical career for Otto's brother Brun, who was a crucial support for Otto throughout his reign. The Saxon nobility (at least putatively) elected their king rather than relying upon primogeniture, and a queen continued to exercise great influence as long as she lived. Thus Henry's son with Mathilda was chosen as ruler rather than his eldest son, Thangmar. Otto I (Otto the Great) became king in 936 upon the death of Henry I, and two years later Thangmar was killed as participant in a rebellion against him. A younger brother, Henry, also rebelled several times and each time returned to favor. Otto made him duke of Bavaria in 947 and ensured that Henry's daughter would not cause problems through an inconvenient marriage by installing her at Gandersheim. This was Gerberga (II), Hrotsvit's abbess.

Otto I limited competition from members of the royal family by giving them significant lands to rule outside of Saxony, his center of royal power. He also used dukedoms and marriages to create personal bonds between the Saxon Liudolfing family and the Frankish Conradine family, thereby expanding his rule. In 939, he betrothed his nine-year-old son Liudolf to Ida, the daughter of a duke who had helped him put down a rebellion in Franconia. After they married in 947, Otto designated Liudolf (II) as sole successor and made him duke of Swabia.[37] The duchy of Lotharingia went to Conrad the Red in 944 in return for his support in suppressing a rebellion, and three years later Otto arranged the marriage of his daughter Liudgard to Conrad. When both Conrad and Liudolf rebelled against Otto in 953 and were deposed as a result, Otto put his brother Brun in place as duke of Lotharingia. Having recently become archbishop of Cologne, Brun provided ecclesiastical, intellectual, and also military leadership. As his father had done, Otto made strategic use of religious institutions for male as well as female offspring. Otto's oldest son, William, was born to a captive Slavic noblewoman in 928, prior to his marriage to Edith. But Otto avoided the Thangmar scenario: William also entered the church and served as archbishop of Mainz from 954 until his death in 968.

Queen Edith died in 946, and in 951 Otto I added Italy to what was now the Ottonian empire by marrying the widow of King Lothar of Italy, Adelheid. Otto I secured the election of their six-year-old son as king in 962 and shortly thereafter himself attained the title Holy Roman Emperor. He and Adelheid remained south of the Alps for the last ten years of his life, from roughly 963-73. Although Pope John III crowned their son as co-emperor in 967 at age 12, Otto II had no independent power while his father lived; instead, the Empress Mathilda, Archibishop Brun of Cologne, and Archbishop William of Mainz controlled the empire in Saxony – his grandmother, uncle, and half-brother.[38] Empress Mathilda, who lived until 968, founded the female monastery Quedlinburg and served as its lay abbess. According to some sources, her son Otto I put her there in order to exercise financial control.[39] He installed his daughter by Adelheid, Mathilda (II), as abbess there, and Empress Adelheid spent most of her time at Quedlinburg after his death. Otto II married Theophanu of Byzantium in 972 and followed family tradition with respect to his daughters, installing Sophia at Gandersheim and Adelheid (II) at Quedlinburg and arranging a marriage to the palatine count Ezzo for Mathilda (III).[40]

Empress Adelheid maintained a controlling influence over Otto II after the death of Otto I in 973. They were estranged for a period beginning in 978 – according to some accounts, due to her expenditures for charity and church building; according to others, because Adelheid took the French side in a conflict between her son and King Lothair of France.[41] They eventually reconciled, and he appointed her viceroy in Italy shortly before his death in 983. Otto II had not secured the succession, but his mother and wife together with Archbishop Willigis of Mainz successfully defended the right of the infant Otto III to the throne. These three served as regents, ruling together with a council of princes: Theophanu held primary power until her death in 991, and then Adelheid took over until Otto III reached majority in 995.[42] Similarly, when Otto III died in 1002, his sisters Sophia and Adelheid (II), now the abbesses of Gandersheim and Quedlinburg, secured the election of Henry II (the grandson of Otto I's brother, Henry of Bavaria). His wife Kundegund became a generous patron of both abbeys and after the death of Henry II dwelt at Kaufungen, her own foundation.[43]

In summary, women such as the empresses Mathilda, Adelheid, and Theophanu functioned as objects of exchange, necessary to cement alliances, and as agents in the transfer of power and land to the emperor. As secure warehouses for young girls and widows as well as those women whose marriages would have created dynastic complications, female monasteries served to contain and control powerful women. Yet they also provided significant freedom and power for the very same women, who were not subject to strict claustration but moved between court and monastery. In addition to their political and social importance, the ruling women of the Ottonian empire were accorded authority and respect in ecclesiastical spheres. They commissioned many of the illuminated manuscripts and processional crosses created during this period.[44] One cannot know the exact truth of the matter: these characterizations come from chronicles that follow their own polemical design. But these women certainly did control large incomes, and did endow religious foundations – and not only the ones with which they were most closely associated. There is no clear reason to discredit stories about generational conflict over their expenditures as evidence of important tensions within the Ottonian ruling class. In addition to financial matters generating narratives of conflict, one can also glimpse tensions lurking behind the marriage narratives. As already noted, the abbess in charge of the young Mathilda (I) at Herford arranged and supervised her marriage to Henry I. Mathilda later intervened when Conrad the Red abducted her granddaughter Liudgard from Quedlinburg, where she was a pupil: although Otto I had arranged the marriage, Conrad wanted it to progress more quickly, and Liudgard expressed the wish to remain with him. Her grandmother successfully insisted upon her return to the abbey, though.[45] The chronicler might conceivably be leaving a rare trace of tenth-century love here, but Liudgard could equally well have wished to get out of Quedlinburg. The only certainty is that Thietmar of Merseburg's narrative records a grandmother's control of a young woman with enclosure at issue – Liudgard was brought back from the public world until the time that her family considered appropriate for the marriage. Hrotsvit tells one story of direct conflict: Henry of Bavaria (the rebellious younger brother of Otto I) tried to force Gerberga (II, her abbess, his daughter) to honor a political betrothal. When her fiancé refused to release her from the arrangement, according to Hrotsvit, Christ intervened and killed him.[46] The trope of divine intervention in support of a woman's chastity echoes the dramas, but in this case the woman is neither immured nor martyred; instead, from 949-1001, she administered what was in essence a principality.

Gandersheim was a valuable property intimately connected to the Ottonian kings, who relied upon personal bonds to govern. In comparison to the Carolingian rulers a century earlier, they had little governmental infrastructure and made less use of written instruments.[47] Surviving evidence suggests that literacy had declined in the tenth century to such an extent that it was primarily the province of the ruling elite and the church, tying these groups more closely as the channels for literate communication.[48] The rulers spent at least half their time traveling and stayed in each place for a few days or a few weeks at most, often at monasteries that provided lodging, food, and similar provisions. Overnight stays at Gandersheim were very likely common (especially from the time of the later Ottonian rulers), given its location at the intersection of two major roads used in the royal itinerary and its proximity to Goslar. The king would have stayed at the monastery itself, where he had special rooms, and the monastic church had a royal gallery. In addition to this sort of accommodation, monasteries generally owed military and monetary contributions. In exchange, they received protection and immunity from the local nobility. Their obligation to the king made it impossible for an Ottonian monastery to relinquish private property and take a vow of poverty; instead, the monastery's property was separated into the abbot or abbess's portion and the fraternal portion, thereby significantly secularizing the abbot or abbess. The monks or nuns provided their portion of service through prayer, and the abbot or abbess provided the material portion of the *servitium regis*. Gandersheim owned many properties outright and had tribute from others, and it was greatly enriched and empowered in the last half of the tenth century. Silver reserves were discovered nearby at Rammelsberg in 968, and Otto III granted Gandersheim the right to coin money in 990.[49]

One might think of this as Gandersheim's silver age, and Hrotsvit wrote her dramas during this period. Because the only certain evidence we have about her life comes from her own writings, precise dates are impossible to determine. Wilson and McNamara suggest that she was born around the time that Otto became king, entered Gandersheim after he became emperor in 962, and wrote her last existing work in the year of his death, 973. Wailes argues that the only temporal certainty is that she was at Gandersheim for some portion of the period when Gerberga (II) was abbess.[50] The plays may have been acted or read aloud at court, but members of the court would just as likely have encountered Hrotsvit and her writing during stays at Gandersheim. Prior to 963, her audiences may have included Otto I and Adelheid – of some interest, she understood Latin, but he did not. Hrotsvit may have had contact with the regents Mathilda (I) and Archbishop William of Mainz prior to their deaths in 968; with Archbishop Brun, who remained regent until 973, when Otto II became emperor; and with Theophanu from 972 onward. But of course the rulers did not travel alone, and scholars were among their companions.[51] In using the scenario of containment to search for traces of the repertoire within the archive, I'm looking for corresponding tropes rather than direct representation. Discord between emperor and empress goes unrecorded by the chroniclers, but they describe widowed empresses' spending as a disruption of harmony with their emperor sons. The empresses were no strangers to Gandersheim, although they were more closely associated with Quedlinberg.

Tensions more directly related to Gandersheim revolved around ecclesiastical oversight, and they erupt in narratives of escape that begin with Sophia, daughter of Otto II and Theophanu. She entered the abbey in 980 and features first as postulant escapee; later, as abbess enforcer. Escape stories record another facet of enclosure, just the sort of contrasting element required to produce harmony, and they all center on a close relationship with Archbishop Willigis of Mainz and his struggle with the bishop of Hildesheim for authority over Gandersheim. Cathedral scholar Thangmar of Hildesheim records in the vita of Bishop Bernward that "even Sophia, against the forceful opposition of [the abbess] Gerburg, and on the urging of Archbishop Willigis, went to the imperial court. Here she remained a year or two and traveled the path of an undisciplined life, which provided the occasion for various rumors."[52] Although Sophia had not yet taken vows, she acted in disregard of her sworn obedience and subordination to the bishop of Hildesheim. Then in 987, at age eleven, Sophia insisted that she be consecrated by the archbishop rather than Bernward, against whose authority her abbess Gerberga had already struggled. In the end, both men participated in her elaborate castimonial ceremony, itself unusual because Gandersheim at this time followed the Aachen rather than the Benedictine rule. The struggle continued: Sophia and Willigis disapproved of Bernward's position as tutor to Otto III, they intervened often in imperial charters, and they accompanied Otto III when he traveled to Italy in 996 to be crowned Holy Roman Emperor. Now twenty years old, Sophia was reported to be "constantly at the side" of the archbishop and to have "lived with him." When a new church was consecrated at Gandersheim, with Gerberga (II) ailing and Sophia presumed as her successor, "the canonesses threw the offertory gifts at the feet of Bishop Bernward during the Mass with 'wild curses' and 'unbelievable fury.'"[53]

Some years later after Sophia had become abbess of Gandersheim, two of her nieces left that convent against her wishes and went to a different religious community in Mainz under the direction of the archbishop's sister. They tore up a letter from the bishop of Hildesheim (at this time no longer Bernward but Godehard) ordering them to return, threatening the messenger's life if he did not depart at once. These two appeared to be following Sophia's example in forming an alliance with Willigis, and to have lived "in a rather familiar way with him." They had dismissed the official escort that Sophia assigned them for an earlier visit. Three other canonesses who had gone to Mainz, supposedly to visit family, joined Sophia's nieces. After she lodged a complaint with the emperor, the five women were returned to Gandersheim and cloistered as nuns. A few months later, though, they were again carried off to Mainz and remained there. One niece stayed in Mainz; the other eventually became abbess at Gandersheim. Pope Sylvester declared in favor of Hildesheim in 1001, but the struggle did not end until Willigis renounced his claim in 1007.[54] Mainz and Hildesheim thus fought over Gandersheim for roughly twenty-seven years, with young women as recurrent figures of disobedience. I propose that the escape narratives play the Thaïs scenario in an imperial key. The descriptions of their behavior never directly allege sexual misconduct, although they hint at it. They do depict members of the royal family as inappropriately public women and their return to enclosure as a reharmonization of the public sphere.

The close relationship between this valuable property and the Ottonian rulers seems to have remained secure, but the stories of escape from Gandersheim offer traces of fracture within the ecclesiastical branch that administered the empire. The six dramas that Hrotsvit wrote there offer further traces, negotiating tensions that its abbesses and canonesses would have experienced in the face of their world's demands and perhaps contributing to the monastery's successful participation in that world. I do not argue here for direct correspondence between her characters or situations and these historical individuals or even that Hrotsvit had a direct message for the women at Gandersheim – although the latter position could perhaps find support. Instead, I see in her dramatic writing and in contemporaneous chronicles traces of a repertoire of embodied practices that simultaneously invest women with worldly power and exercise a shaky control over that power through physical enclosure. The Thaïs scenario enacts a particular sort of enclosure, the restoration of harmony after its disruption by a public woman who knows her own mind, a harmonization in which she willingly participates. Unlike Mary and Thaïs, the Ottonian abbess gave up neither money nor power, even though she acquiesced to certain limits. Hrotsvit's plays are not about love or even about lust, but about money and power.

Notes

1. *The Plays of Hrotsvit of Gandersheim*, translated by Katharina Wilson (New York: Garland Publishing, 1989), 3. Scholars often refer to this play as *Pafnutius*, but I will use Wilson's titles as well as her spelling of the playwright's name and include citations to this source parenthetically within the text, omitting the slashes that indicate line breaks.

2. Regula Meyer Evitt, "Incest Disguised: Ottonian Influence at Gandersheim and Hrotsvit's *Abraham*," *Comparative Drama* 41.3 (2007): 349-69.

3. For a more fully developed argument about the tenth-century practice of reading bodies as accurate signs in trial by ordeal and in Hrotsvit's virgin martyr plays, see Marla Carlson, "Impassive Bodies: Hrotsvit Stages Martyrdom," *Theatre Journal* 50.4 (1998): 473-87. The present article builds upon my earlier argument that Hrotsvit structures her plays differently from Terence or from post-Renaissance Western playwrights because she has a different understanding of God's involvement in the physical world.

4. Evitt begins by noting Wilson's euphemistic translation of *turpia lasciviarum incesta feminarum* as "shameless acts of lascivious women," proposing instead "defiling incest of lascivious women." She goes on to offer a clear and concise discussion of Ottonian dynastic practices and changes to canon law during this period with respect to permissible degrees of consanguinity in marriage: "Incest Disguised," 349-53.

5. Diana Taylor, *The Archive and the Repertoire: Performing Cultural Memory in the Americas* (Durham: Duke University Press, 2003), 19. One of Taylor's most easily grasped examples is the scenario of "discovery" that places Europeans in a position of power (narrative and otherwise) within "New World" encounters.

6. See, e.g., Piyali Sur, "Safety in the Urban Outdoors: Women Negotiating Fear of Crime in the City of Kolkata," *Journal of International Women's Studies* 15.2 (2014): 212-26; Robin Wilson, "When Does Unwanted Sex Become Rape?" *Chronicle of Higher Education* 61.19 (2015): A9.

7. See, e.g., Sharon S. Oselin, "Leaving the Streets: Transformation of Prostitute Identity Within the Prostitute Rehabilitation Program," *Deviant Behavior* 30 (2009): 379-406; Chinyere Ogbonna-McGruder, Michael R. Miller, and Eric Martin, "Analysis of Recidivism Rate of Magdalene Rehabilitation Program for Prostitution," *Journal of Global Intelligence & Policy* 5.9 (2012): 11-29.

8. Anneke B. Mulder-Bakker, foreword to *Anchorites, Wombs and Tombs: Intersections of Gender and Enclosure in the Middle Ages*, ed. Liz Herbert McAvoy and Mari Hughes-Edwards (Cardiff: University of Wales Press, 2005), 1-5.

9. Both the novel and the 1911 dramatic adaptation by Paul Wilstach are currently available on Google Books, as is Oswald Robert Kuehne, "A Study of the Thaïs Legend with Special Reference to Hrothsvitha's *Paphnutius*," (Ph.D. Diss., University of Pennsylvania, 1922), which discusses France's novel at 93-99. Although the *Thaïs* play is the centerpiece of his dissertation, Kuehne calls it "mediocre in comparison" to *The Fall and Repentance of Mary* (75).

10. Aristotle, *Poetics*, trans. Richard Janko (Indianapolis: Hackett, 1987), 50a15-23, 33-34.

11. See Katharina M. Wilson, *Hrotsvit of Gandersheim: The Ethics of Authorial Stance* (Leiden: E.J. Brill, 1988), 54-9.

12. They encountered it in Jennifer Wise's introduction to the play in *Broadview Anthology of Drama*, concise edition, ed. Craig S. Walker and Jennifer Wise (Broadview, 2005), 89-90.

13. David Chamberlain, "Musical Imagery and Musical Learning in Hrotsvit," in *Hrotsvit of Gandersheim, Rara Avis in Saxonia? A Collection of Essays*, edited by Katharina M. Wilson (Ann Arbor, Mich.: MARC Pub. Co., 1987), 91. Chamberlain explicates Hrotsvit's highly original development of musical philosophy drawn primarily from Boethius' *Consolation of Philosophy*, but also from Prudentius' *Psychomachia* and the figure of *Harmonia* in Martianus Capella. See "Musical Learning and Dramatic Action in Hrotsvit's 'Pafnutius,'" *Studies in Philology* 77.4 (1980): 322-3.

14. Although one might consider the brief epitomes that precede Hrotsvit's plays in the primary manuscript to be her prologues, they are of dubious provenance. See Stephen Wailes, *Spirituality and Politics in the Works of Hrotsvit of Gandersheim* (Selinsgrove: Susquehanna University Press, 2006), 21, with a review of relevant scholarship at 241 n12. Chamberlain refers to the first scene as a "learned Prologue" ("Musical Imagery," 319), and I differ with him only in his choice of this terminology – he clearly does not have in mind the Terentian-style prologue.

15. Donatus, "On Comedy," in *Classical and Medieval Literary Criticism*, ed. Alex Preminger, Jr., O.B. Hardison and Kevin Kerrane (New York: Frederick Ungar, 1974), 307.

16. Chamberlain, "Musical Imagery," 330.

17. Ibid., 332.

18. See Carlson, "Impassive Bodies," and sources cited therein for discussion of Hrotsvit's self-deprecating rhetoric.

19. Evanthius, "On Drama," in *Classical and Medieval Literary Criticism*, 305; Donatus, "On Comedy," 308.

20. Chamberlain, "Musical Imagery," 334-5, provides a detailed analysis of the musical terms that Hrotsvit uses here.

21. Jocelyn Wogan-Brown, "Chaste Bodies: Frames and Experiences," in *Framing Medieval Bodies*, ed. Sarah Kay and Miri Rubin (Manchester: Manchester University Press, 1994), 27, citing *The English Text of the Ancrene Riwle: Ancrene Wisse*, ed. J.R.R. Tolkien, EETS OS 249 (London: 1962): f. 4a/16-17; *Anchoritic Spirituality: Ancrene Wisse and Associated Works*, trans. Anne Savage and Nicholas Watson (New York: 1991), 51.

22. Bella Millett, *Ancrene Wisse = Guide for Anchoresses: A Translation Based on Cambridge, Corpus Christi College, MS 402* (Exeter: University of Exeter Press, 2009), 30-31, paragraphs 19-20.

23. Evanthius, "On Drama," 305; Donatus, "On Comedy," 308. Note that in this context the term "catastrophe" has none of its now more familiar connotations of extreme misfortune.

24. Stephen L. Wailes, "Beyond Virginity: Flesh and Spirit in the Plays of Hrotsvit of Gandersheim," *Speculum* 76.1 (2001): 18; and Evitt, "Incest Disguised," 365 n5, alerted me to these recluses.

25. Liutbirg, Hathumoda, and Frederick S. Paxton, *Anchoress and Abbess in Ninth-Century Saxony: The Lives of Liutbirga of Wendhausen and Hathumoda of Gandersheim* (Washington, D.C.: Catholic University of America Press, 2009), 100-1.

26. Paxton, *Anchoress and Abbess*, 103-14. Also see, for both Liutbirg and Wiborada, Gabriela Signori, "Anchorites in German-Speaking Regions," in *Anchoritic Traditions of Medieval Europe*, ed. Liz Herbert McAvoy (Woodbridge: Boydell, 2010), 48-52.

27. Sarah Gallick, *The Big Book of Women Saints* (New York: HarperCollins, 2007), 134.

28. Jane Tibbetts Schulenberg, *Forgetful of their Sex: Female Sanctity and Society, ca. 500-1100* (Chicago: University of Chicago, 1998), 293-4.

29. Paul Lendvai, *The Hungarians: A Thousand Years of Victory in Defeat* (Princeton: Princeton University Press, 2003), 7-8.

30. Tom Licence, *Hermits and Recluses in English Society, 950-1200* (Oxford: Oxford University Press, 2011), 67-71. Licence suggests a connection between anchoritism at St. Gall and its eponymous saint, an Irish *peregrinus* and anchorite. Eleventh-century chronicler Marianus Scotus writes of other Irish recluses in Hesse and Saxony, all male, and he finished his own life in a cell at Mainz cathedral.

31. The only other instance in the six plays occurs in *Drusiana and Calimachus*. The heroine has prayed to die rather than to ruin Calimachus, who lusts after her. Although her prayer is granted, the young man rapes her corpse and then dies from fear when a snake suddenly appears. The Apostle John revives Drusiana, then both advises her and empowers her to bring her seducer Calimachus back to life in order to save his soul. Hrotsvit also consistently dramatizes the Christian act of giving up material possessions, which includes giving up the physical body through either martyrdom or mortification. To consider only the two harlot-redemption plays: both Mary and Thaïs dispose of their ill-gotten wealth as they leave their lives as sex workers. Mary wishes to give hers to the poor or to the church, but her spiritual guide Abraham objects that "it is neither sanctioned nor acceptable that gifts be given to God which were acquired through sin and are impure" (88). Thaïs herself knows that she must burn her possessions, and her ultimate reward after three years' penance is to leave her material body. Pafnutius is with her, and his final prayer describes the dissolution of the "diverse parts of this human being" so that the soul rejoins the immateriality of God and the body returns to "ashes and dirt" (122).

32. In particular, see Ulrike Wiethaus, "Body and Empire in the Works of Hrotsvit of Gandersheim," *Journal of Medieval and Early Modern Studies* 34.1 (2004): 41-63; Phyllis R. Brown and Stephen L. Wailes, "Hrotsvit and Her World," in *A Companion to Hrotsvit of Gandersheim (Fl. 960): Contextual and Interpretive Approaches*, ed. Brown and Wailes (Leiden: Brill, 2013), 3-21.

33. For a overview of Liudolfing monasticism and inheritance, see Sean Gilsdorf's introduction to *Queenship and Sanctity: The Lives of Mathilda and the Epitaph of Adelheid* (Washington, D.C.: Catholic University of America Press, 2004), 23-28. He presents a concise dynastic history focused on the Empresses Mathilda and Adelheid at 2-7.

34. Jo Ann McNamara, *Sisters in Arms: Catholic Nuns through Two Millennia* (Cambridge: Harvard University Press, 1996), 194.

35. Karl Leyser, *Rule and Conflict in an Early Medieval Society* (Bloomington: Indiana University Press, 1979), 52-64. Patrick Geary notes that similar convents had been established in western Europe during the previous century. *Phantoms of Remembrance: Memory and Oblivion at the End of the First Millennium* (Princeton: Princeton University Press, 1994), 66-7.

36. John W. Bernhardt, *Itinerant Kingship and Royal Monasteries in Early Medieval Germany c. 936-1075* (Cambridge: Cambridge University Press, 1993), 14.

37. Bernhardt, *Itinerant Kingship*, 21.

38. Timothy Reuter, *Germany in the Early Middle Ages c. 800-1056* (London: Longman, 1991), 155-9.

39. McNamara says that Otto I "forced" his mother Mathilda into a convent "because he resented her extravagant charities" and he "confiscated her dotal lands:" *Sisters in Arms*, 195. Also see Gilsdorf, *Queenship and Sanctity*, 14-15 and sources cited therein.
40. Wilson, *Ethics of Authorial Stance*, 150; McNamara, *Sisters in Arms*, 188-90.
41. Gilsdorf attributes the first explanation to Syrus's vita of Maiolus of Cluny. Odilo of Cluny explicitly deigns to give particulars of the disagreement in his Epitaph of Adelheid: see Gilsdorf, *Queenship and Sanctity*, 14-15 at 133.
42. "Adelaide of Italy," *The 1911 Classic Encyclopedia*, 31 Aug 2006, http://www.1911encyclopedia.org, accessed 16 Oct 2011. For a more complete treatment of the relationship between Adelheid and Theophanu, see Gilsdorf, *Queenship and Sanctity*, 11-14.
43. McNamara, *Sisters in Arms*, 196.
44. Leyser, *Rule and Conflict*, 49-50. Both Leyser (at 56) and McNamara (at 181) note that for some tenth-century Saxon families, the historical record consists primarily of the lavish religious foundations of their womenfolk.
45. *Ottonian Germany: The Chronicon of Thietmar of Merseburg*, ed. and trans. David Warner (Manchester, UK: Manchester University Press, 2001).
46. McNamara, *Sister in Arms*, 193; Linda A. McMillin, "The Audiences of Hrotsvit," in *A Companion*, ed. Steven L. Wailes and Phyllis R. Brown, 314-15, quoting "Hrotsvit of Gandersheim, The Establishment of the Monastery at Gandersheim" (*Primordia*), trans. Thomas Head, orig. trans. Mary Bernadine Bergman, in *Medieval Hagiography: An Anthology*, ed. Head (New York: Routledge, 2001), 248.
47. Bernhardt, *Itinerant Kingship*, 51.
48. Karl Leyser, *Communications and Power in Medieval Europe: The Carolingian and Ottonian Centuries* (London: The Hambledon Pres, 1994), 195-6.
49. Bernhardt, *Itinerant Kingship*, 48, 151-3, 85-6, 154-61.
50. Wilson, *Ethics of Authorial Stance*, 150; McNamara, *Sisters in Arms*, 189; Wailes, *Spirituality and Politics*, 17.
51. Chamberlain argues that the discourse on musical philosophy in the *Thaïs* play responded to a wish of the learned friends to whom Hrotsvit addressed her dedicatory epistles for her plays to include more philosophical learning. He makes a particular argument for Gunzo of Novara as the source of her interest in Boethius. "Musical Imagery," 321 n9-10.
52. As quoted by Heinrich Fichtenau, *Living in the Tenth Century: Mentalities and Social Orders*, trans. Peter Geary (Chicago: University of Chicago Press, 1991), 228.
53. Fichtenau, *Living in the Tenth Century*, 228-9, quoting from the *vita* of St. Bernward.
54. See Horace K. Mann and Johannes Hollnsteiner, *The Lives of the Popes in the Early Middle Ages*, 2nd ed., vol. 5 (London: K. Paul, 1925), 95-8; Francis Joseph Tschan, *Saint Bernward of Hildesheim*, vol. 1 (Publications in Mediaeval Studies, The University of Notre Dame), 157-99.

"Since I have your good leave to go away": Negotiating desire in *The Merchant of Venice*
Erin Weinberg

*O*n the early English stage, heteronormativity was an emerging phenomenon, not a stubbornly entrenched social norm. In *The Merchant of Venice,* Shakespeare depicts a struggle between the neo-platonic superiority of male friendship and the early modern shift towards privileging marriage as a superior form of intimacy. The competing affinities within the romance plot demonstrate this struggle with desires that compete with the married state.[1] Valerie Traub argues that this nuanced approach to desire shows how "the sex/gender/sexuality system as represented by Shakespeare was not continuous, unified, cohesive, or closed, but fractured, unstable, contradictory, open to negotiation and resistance."[2] I apply Traub's argument to the play's romance plot to make a case for desire as indeed "open to negotiation"; the original marriage bond between Bassanio and Portia fails when it fails to negotiate what James M. Bromley calls "alternative forms of relationality."[3] These alternate forms are essential to the fulfillment of their desires, and threaten the emerging paradigm of heteronormativity: Bassanio's affections are fractured between Portia and his homoerotic desire for Antonio, whereas Portia negotiates an alternate form of relationality for herself, yearning for an intellectual liberty beyond the confines of patriarchal gender norms. While many critics have suggested that the play's final scene represents a patchwork resolution in the face of Bassanio's infidelity towards both of his lovers, I argue that Shakespeare's conclusion succeeds in supporting marital cohesion between Bassanio and Portia because it does not reject Antonio's claim on Bassanio's affections *or* Portia's cross-dressing to exercise intellectual freedom. The renewed marriage bond is promising precisely *because* it accommodates the desires that Bassanio and Portia cannot physically fulfill for each other. As such, the play's resolution negotiates an affective nexus in which alternate forms of relationality should be understood as not impeding, but instead enabling the shift to increased marital intimacy on the early stage.

Bassanio reciprocates Antonio's desire, both sexual and companionate. This deliberately "queered"[4] reading builds on the critical foundation of Traub, Bromley, and Alan Sinfield, whose "against the grain"[5] mode of analysis I use to highlight Bassanio and Antonio's homoerotic relationship as struggling against the romance structure. As romance hero, Bassanio undergoes a series of tests to purge all irresponsibility, proving himself worthy of a marriage bond, property ownership, and futurity: the transmission of his family line and capital through the production of offspring. His homoerotic desire for Antonio is at odds with his desire for all that marriage to Portia promises; these desires seem contradictory and thereby impossible to achieve concurrently. However, by performing an "against the grain" reading, I will show how, if accommodated, these alternate forms of relationality have the potential to support the otherwise unstable shift towards heteronormativity.

Bassanio's intimate relationship with Antonio is based on their physical and emotional closeness. Gail Kern Paster's well-known body of work shows that the Galenic model of medicine followed by early modern thinkers situates the emotions in the body.[6] Affect, accordingly, was thought to be manifest in bodily responses to stimuli. The profound intimacy between Antonio and Bassanio is manifest in their bodily permeability, a shared interiority that Shakespeare often depicts in his married characters. Their proximity is threatened when Bassanio pledges to leave Venice in pursuit of "a lady richly left" (1.1.160).[7] Anticipating Bassanio's departure, Antonio opens the play with the line: "In sooth I know not why I am so sad" (1.1.1). This language of elusive sadness reflects his struggle to negotiate the alternate forms of relationality that Bassanio desires, but Antonio cannot personally accommodate. Bassanio's companions identify Antonio's melancholy as lovesickness, jumping to the immediate conclusion: "Why then, you are in love" (1.1.46). Antonio interrupts Salarino with the exclamation, "Fie, Fie!" (1.1.46), but this barely verbal response does not provide an explicit answer. His secrecy is worth considering, however, since these friends seem aware yet unaffected by his feelings towards Bassanio. Gratiano hints at Antonio's surprising discretion when he asks: "Why should a man whose blood is warm within / Sit like his grandsire cut in alabaster?" (1.1.83-84). He grapples with the call of his "warm" blood because it could lead him to continue acting on his homoerotic desire when Bassanio has indicated a desire to marry Portia. Antonio's short sentences and shorter temper express his struggle with the prospect of letting his "hot" blood grow "cold" upon Bassanio's withdrawal from his proximity and, Antonio fears, his affections.

Bassanio, likewise, expresses his struggle with the alternate forms of relationality that threaten his intimacy with Antonio and pull him towards Portia. When he tells his friend, "To you, Antonio, / I owe the most in money and in love" (1.1.129-30), his words portend the fate of their relationship: with his "money" locked in debt and Antonio's tied up at sea, their "love" is not strong enough to keep them together. Shakespeare's yoking of "money" and "love" nonetheless indicates Bassanio's ambivalence with the prospect of severing his sexual bond with Antonio in order to "get clear of all the debts I owe" (1.1.133). Bassanio adds the word "love" to his pledge, showing that despite their current insolvency, there is no lack of romantic affinity between them. Despite this ambivalence, Bassanio leaves for Belmont, knowing that in order to be financially solvent, he must marry Portia, thereby binding himself to her in futurity.

Antonio cannot literally accommodate Bassanio's financial needs, but he rhetorically pledges himself in vain substitution. He responds to Bassanio's consolations with the pledge: "My purse, my person, my extremest means / Lie all unlocked to your occasions" (1.1.137-8). Antonio's offering of his "purse" is dangerous because he cannot be sure that his own money will multiply at sea. This leads him to risk his life in return for Shylock's purse of ducats, a hateful distortion of Antonio's bond of love with Bassanio. The flesh bond is Antonio's attempt to overcome his inability to make his money multiply, the affluence that would prevent Bassanio's pursuit of a bond more physically demanding than Antonio can fulfill: the bond of futurity. His deficiency is implied in the word "purse," symbolizing the scrotum[8] as an inadequate means to establish futurity with Bassanio. Antonio's offering attempts to compete against Bassanio's ring exchange with Portia, a symbolic sacrifice of her maidenhood through the bonds of marriage. However, the difference between a "purse" and a "ring" is that while the former offers sterility, the latter, symbolizing Portia's fertile womb, grants progeny. Antonio tries to rhetorically negotiate the physical limits of their homoerotic relationship but these attempts are in vain.

Like Antonio, Portia expresses a sense of suffering over the limits imposed on her sex. These limits are based on patriarchal biases about gender: what the female sex is presumed to be constitutionally capable or incapable of performing. Portia's character is sharp-witted from the start, showing that she has an intellect perfectly capable of being cultivated through the same methods as educated men. Devoid of the opportunity to exercise that intellect, her opening lines mirror Antonio's sadness. When she says, "my little body is aweary of this great world" (1.2.1-2), Shakespeare depicts the weariness of her agile mind being confined by the social rules inscribed to femininity. Without being able to pursue the intellectual liberty that she finds a more stimulating and authentic expression of herself, Portia's struggle exemplifies Traub's argument that "We have no unmediated access to our bodies; our bodies, our subjectives, our desires and anxieties, are constituted in relation to social processes."[9]

The casket test limits Portia's choice of suitors to men with wits sharp enough to match her own. Although the test may be beneficial in narrowing the suitors to the least ridiculous of the bunch, it also restricts Portia's own desires from influencing her marriage prospects. No matter how well intentioned, the process nonetheless implies that, as a woman, Portia is incapable of making a prudent decision over how to direct her body and her fortunes. She expresses feelings of claustrophobia from this symbolic entombment, lamenting to Nerissa:

> …a hot temper leaps o'er a cold decree – …O me, the word 'choose'! I may neither choose who I would, nor refuse who I dislike, so is the will of a living daughter curbed by the will of a dead father. Is it not hard, Nerissa, that I cannot choose one nor refuse none? (1.2.16-22)

The caskets that contain Portia's freedom simultaneously restrict her agency. No matter how much she wants to "choose" or "refuse," she is unable to because the legal system does not recognize her intellectual capacity. Despite her father's attempt to choose the "best" husband for her, like Antonio, Portia is "cut in alabaster." Her "hot temper" shows a desire for something other than the marital commitments that await her, yet Portia lacks the right to refuse the victor's claim to her maidenhead. Symbolized as "the cold decree," her father's will prevents her from choosing, even though she remains alive as her father's body grows cold.

Until the romance test is concluded, Portia's own portion is stagnant: it contains tremendous monetary value, but is valueless until she binds herself to a man through marriage and the conjugation of that bond. Her struggle brings to mind Lee Edelman's theory of the abstract of future offspring, for whom people make great sacrifices at the expense of their own present happiness. He writes:

> That figural Child alone embodies the citizen as an ideal, entitled to claim full rights to its future share in the nation's good, although always at the cost of limiting the rights "real" citizens are allowed.[10]

Portia knows that bearing children is her responsibility, and is the course of action that must follow a suitor's victory over the casket test. She expresses no joy in the prospect until Bassanio arrives at Belmont. Nerissa enthusiastically expresses her attraction towards him, telling Portia: "he of all the men that ever my foolish eyes looked upon was the best deserving a fair lady" (1.2.96-97). Portia agrees, saying, "I remember him well, and I remember him worthy of thy praise," and consents to "see / Quick Cupid's post that comes so mannerly" (2.9.98-99). Portia's utterances show more reserve than Nerissa's effusions, as her desires are limited to hopes for a man more "mannerly" than the suitors she scornfully surveys in Act 1, scene 2. Her intentions to "see" if Bassanio is "worthy of praise" shows less erotic inclination and more of desire to see if Bassanio's "manners" are compatible with her own.

Despite her struggles with the means of "choosing" her spouse, Portia expresses undeniable joy at Bassanio's success in the casket test. In an aside, she declares:

> O love, be moderate; allay thy ecstasy,
> In measure rain thy joy, scant this excess!
> I feel too much thy blessing: make it less,
> For fear I surfeit. (3.2.111-14)

Shakespeare's use of an aside suggests that he is portraying Portia's sincere, unbridled assent to the match. Her expressions are now effusive: "rash," "doubtful," "ecsta[tic]," and "joy[ful]"; they suggest that she does indeed feel affinity towards Bassanio, and that his victory influences her "love" for him. This indicates her appreciation of Bassanio's compatible "manners" as proven by his successful answers to her father's riddles, and her joy at the "blessing" of freedom from the test that entombed her desire. However, this affinity is not necessarily rooted in sexual desire.

Portia uses the marriage bond as an opportunity to advance her own freedom. After her initial effusions, she regains composure and addresses Bassanio in terms that subordinate herself to her new patriarch. She tells him:

> the full sum of me
> Is sum of something: which to term in gross
> Is an unlessoned girl, unschooled, unpractised;
> Happy in this, she is not yet so old
> But she may learn; happier than this,
> She is not bred so dull but she can learn;
> Happiest of all is that her gentle spirit
> Commits itself to yours to be directed
> As from her lord, her governor, her king. (3.2.157-65)

Portia's self-deprecation is ironic, considering how witty she proves herself in dialogue with Nerissa and her suitors. Her subordination is strategic, manipulating Bassanio into being complicit towards fulfilling her desire for intellectual liberty. Portia repeats the word "learn," which expresses a yearning to develop her intellect with the freedom held by men. Her use of the word "governor" implies the early modern definition of "One who has charge of a young man's education,"[11] which shows Portia posturing herself as relying on Bassanio's benevolence as "her governor" to enable her to become "much better." In removing her education as a threat to his mastery as "governor" of the household, Portia subordinates her own intelligence in order to gain the freedom to cultivate it further.

Negotiating with Bassanio's authority as husband and bearer of her fortunes, Portia's rhetoric subtly shifts the power from Bassanio to herself. Through her offer of the "full sum of me," Shakespeare links Portia's pledge to Shylock's justification of usury based on the allegory of the "fulsome ewe" that multiplies through natural procreation (1.3.68-82). Marc Shell suggests that "a fertile ewe, unlike a monetary principal, needs a potent ram to generate offspring;"[12] however, the potent ram is likewise powerless without an ewe to impregnate. In order for Bassanio's fortunes to multiply, Portia reminds him, he must procreate with her. This physical permeability would reflect and support their financial permeability through marriage. Yet, she threatens, if Bassanio loses or gives away her ring, the symbol of her chastity, "Let it presage the ruin of your love, / And be my vantage to exclaim on you" (3.2.173-4). Because the ring represents the chastity of the womb that will bear his children, Portia's "exclamation" is implied as her refusal to share his marriage bed, which would prevent the transmission of their shared fortunes from generation to generation. In what began as a speech of subordination, Portia shifts the power structure to claim her own agency in the marriage bond. This shift reveals Portia's emerging feelings of empowerment as a result of her liberation from the casket test. Although she could not "choose" or "refuse" the man to win her ring and the womb it represents, Portia assumes her own agency by declaring that this symbol of "traditional wifely submission"[13] that she has given Bassanio is nonetheless hers to take away.

As the new master of the house, Bassanio is in power, but he recognizes that he is beholden to Portia's beneficence for transforming him from a man in debt to a man of fortune. He expresses his gratitude, saying:

> Madam, you have bereft me of all words.
> Only my blood speaks to you in my veins,
> And there is such confusion in my powers
> As after some oration fairly spoke
> By a belovèd prince there doth appear
> Among the buzzing, pleasèd multitude,
> Where every something being blent together
> Turns to a wild of nothing, save of joy
> Expressed and not expressed. (3.2.175-85)

Bassanio's response conveys his emotional conflict between pledging an eternal bond to one who can clear all his debts, and continuing to feel profoundly for another. Like Portia's effusions, Bassanio's feelings on the occasion of his betrothal are not simple, but "unstable, contradictory, and open to negotiation." By verbalizing his sense of speechlessness, Bassanio shows that he is not indeed "bereft…of all words," but is affecting an emotional shift that is not supported by conspicuous physical evidence. Bassanio calls on his own speechlessness to "express" his joy in the implications of uniting himself with Portia, but his speech nonetheless represents his troubled state. What he leaves deliberately "not expressed" is this destabilizing factor: the affinity for Antonio that he cannot forget, despite not mentioning him to Portia. It is Bassanio's emotional "confusion," this lingering homoerotic passion, which betrays the instability of his marriage bond from the moment of betrothal.

Bassanio's feelings for Antonio do not cease despite the physical fracture of their relationship. The "unexpressed" "wild of nothing" that Bassanio speaks of is his desire for Antonio, which must come to "nothing" as a result of their inability to reproduce through money or offspring. Bassanio knows that "nothing" can be created from sharing two "purses" without the necessary "ring," and Shakespeare exemplifies these contradictory impulses through Bassanio's foil, Gratiano. When Gratiano announces his own engagement to Nerissa, Bassanio declares, "Our feast shall be much honoured in your marriage" (3.2.212). His response is mannered, attending to the marriage ritual, rather than any erotic desire behind it. Gratiano, by contrast, is focused on the erotic potential of the consummation that follows. His challenge, "We'll play with them the first boy for a thousand ducats" (3.2.213-4), represents the shift towards privileging marriage as a superior form of intimacy. Gratiano's bawdy joke gestures towards a patriarchal dominance in which sexual reproduction is privileged as a man's priority: a responsibility that should be undertaken with joy. Bassanio conceals his contradictory desires by focusing on his legal responsibilities rather than his sexual duties. Gratiano's jibe poses a reminder that words are insufficient: the bond is only fulfilled when it is consummated.

Despite Gratiano's reminder, Portia and Bassanio do not immediately consummate their marriage. This is due to Salerio's arrival immediately following the vow exchange, with a message from Antonio. Bassanio's speechlessness towards the contents of Antonio's letter contrasts with his effusiveness only moments earlier. Here, he does not verbalize his emotions; they are manifest in his actual rather than self-professed speechlessness, as well as an abrupt change in countenance. Portia notices this physical embodiment of grief and says:

> There are some shrewd contents in yond same paper
> That steals the colour from Bassanio's cheek:
> Some dear friend dead, else nothing in the world
> Could turn so much the constitution
> Of any constant man. (3.2.242-6)

Bassanio's affective shift shows Portia that he requites Antonio's desire. The fact that Antonio's worries can drain the blood from Bassanio's face reveals the enduring strength of their shared interiority, even with Bassanio stepping out of Venice and into an alternate bond. Although Bassanio had told Portia, "Only my blood speaks to you in my veins" (3.2.176), it is clear that his blood is not closed off to Antonio. When Portia suggests that only death could "turn so much the constitution / Of any constant man," she begins to recognize the instability in her own relationship, due to Bassanio's emotional "constancy" towards Antonio.

What marks Bassanio's interiorized desire with Antonio as threatening to the emerging heteronormative social order is that it is strong enough to halt his pursuit of futurity with Portia. Bassanio's *deus ex machina* arrives onstage long before Portia appears in the courtroom to save Antonio's life: Salerio's arrival in the seconds following the ring pledge saves Bassanio from initiating his bond of futurity with Portia. Regaining composure after reading Antonio's letter, Bassanio expresses feelings contradictory to those that he had most recently affected to Portia, telling her: "I have engaged myself to a dear friend" (3.2.200). Portia reacts to Bassanio's split affinity not with anger or shame, but with magnanimity. She insists on Bassanio's pursuit through the imperative, "Come away, / For you shall hence upon your wedding day" (3.2.309-10) – so long as Bassanio first "go with me to church and call me wife" (3.2.302). Rather than being eager to consummate his marriage, Bassanio quickly assents to her suggestion of aborting their wedding night. He tells Portia: "Since I have your good leave to go away, / I will make haste" (3.2.321-2). Bassanio focuses on Portia's "good leave" in order to tactfully displace his own desire to absent himself. Nonetheless, he makes his desire to protect Antonio conspicuous in the following line, saying that he will "make haste." Unlike Portia's subordination of herself for the sake of their "figural Child," Bassanio shows a greater sense of urgency towards Antonio's immediate physical and emotional needs.

Bassanio's abandonment of Portia confirms their unstable relationship: legally bound, but physically unconsummated. He closes the scene by telling her: "till I come again / No bed shall e'er be guilty of my stay / Nor rest be interposer 'twixt us twain" (3.2.322-4). At first glance, Bassanio seems to be endorsing the patriarchal expectations of a heterosexual marital relationship. Yet, considering that he has just completed reading Antonio's letter, Bassanio's assertion, "No bed shall e'er be guilty of my stay / Nor rest be interposer 'twixt us twain," should be understood as directed towards Antonio, rather than Portia. The "rest" that Bassanio rejects is every moment or object that "interposes" between himself and his reunion with Antonio. The threatening "interposer" in this speech, then, is Portia, the one with whom Bassanio will not allow himself to "rest" until he feels that Antonio is out of danger. This ambiguity is highlighted by the fact that Bassanio does not confirm his own "stay" in Portia's "bed" by claiming her maidenhood immediately after their exchange of vows. This urgency to save his friend succeeding against any urgency to consummate his marriage confirms Bromley's assertion that early modern plays do not unilaterally privilege heterosexual coupling, but rather "raise questions about marriage as a locus of affection by persistently mourning the friendship that marriage would replace."[14]

It is surprising that a wife would assent to being abandoned on her wedding night, her own fecundity resisted in favor of the "the friendship that marriage would replace." Further overlooked, moreover, is Portia's own vehemence that Bassanio leave Belmont. Instead of begging her husband to stay, Portia tells Bassanio: "never shall you lie by Portia's side / With an unquiet soul" (3.2.304-5). By saying "never," she, too, is complicit in the indefinite delay of their consummation. Her desire for her husband to sleep "by Portia's side" lacks the sexual suggestion of Bassanio's apostrophe to Antonio that "nor rest be interposer twixt us twain." "Twixt" is a word that suggests interconnectedness, a bond of intertwined bodies and emotions, whereas Portia's vision of her marriage bed is symbolic of her desire for equal status in the marriage: contributing alongside each other rather than endorsing male dominance and female subordination. Portia demonstrates a degree of sexual detachment from Bassanio, showing that she privileges their partnership of minds above their partnership of bodies.

Portia's demand that Bassanio leaves Belmont on their wedding night shows a conspicuous lack of romantic feeling on her part. Lorenzo takes note of this, telling her: "You have a noble and a true conceit / Of god-like amity, which appears most strongly / In bearing thus the absence of your lord" (3.4.2-4). Suggesting that she "bears" Bassanio's absence confirms the public perception that it is indeed a sexual rejection, and one that Portia could react to negatively, without deserving blame. Whereas Sinfield claims that "the seriousness of the love between Antonio and Bassanio is manifest, above all, in Portia's determination to contest it,"[15] I argue that Portia proves her acceptance of Bassanio's devotion to Antonio by personally suggesting that he leave Belmont before consummating the marriage. Portia qualifies her magnanimity by saying:

> for in companions
> That do converse and waste the time together,
> Whose souls do bear an equal yoke of love,
> There must be needs a like proportion
> Of lineaments, of manners, and of spirit;
> Which makes me think that this Antonio,
> Being the bosom lover of my lord,
> Must needs be like my lord. (3.4.11-17)

Portia speaks of Antonio's relationship with Bassanio as one would refer to a married couple. Suggesting that the two male souls "do bear an equal yoke of love," she acknowledges her husband's interior bond with Antonio, even though she herself has exchanged vows to share Bassanio's "yoke." By saying, "Being the bosom lover of my lord, / [Antonio] Must needs be like my lord," Portia implies that, by virtue of overlapping bonds, Antonio's needs become her own.

It is necessary to examine Portia's stakes in her determined resignation of her wedding night. Once Portia is married, she is free of the casket test. Her joy in this freedom shows that she is not invested in the potential for futurity, but rather, the other opportunities she can pursue in the moments after the vows but before consummation. When she assumes the mantle of Balthazar, the young lawyer sent to represent Antonio, Portia engages in an opportunity to explore gender on her own terms. Outside of the control of her father's will or a consummated marriage, Portia tells herself: "Now, Balthazar – /As I have ever found thee honest-true, / So let me find thee still" (3.4.45-47). When Portia seeks out Balthazar, she is speaking of the masculinity that she "finds" within herself. By saying "still," she shows that this is a side of herself that she has reached for in the past and found "honest-true": a more genuine expression of her gender identity than she is able to exercise under patriarchal constraints, such as the casket test that removed her free will from the process of finding her a husband. While Bassanio is pursuing his homoerotic bond with Antonio, Portia is cultivating a bond with the masculine side of herself. By assenting to the indefinite delay of consummation, Portia takes advantage of her single opportunity to experience this alternate form of relationality.

While it is customary to explore Portia's cross-dressing in terms of her own sexual desire or jealousy, I contend that Portia's cross-dressing indicates a desire that is not sexual, but intellectual. By inverting her sex through cross-dressing, Portia explores the social opportunities from which she, as a woman, is restricted. Her desire for intellectual liberation resonates in Act 3, Scene 2, when she says: "She is not bred so dull but she can learn." Portia denounces dullness in favor of intellectual pursuits; even in that speech of self-deprecation, she shows a determination to intellectually better herself beyond the socially constructed limits of her sex. Instead of being silent and obedient to the whims of her father and husband, Portia seizes the opportunity to be public and active, privileges of men. Her desire is reflected in her decision to immediately leave the privacy of Belmont, not for the silence and obedience of monastic life, where she falsely claims to endure her husband's absence, but for Venice: one of the most cosmopolitan cities in early modern Europe.

The Venetian courtroom is a setting that unites Portia's desire for the freedom masculinity entails with her desire for the public expression of intellect. Jesting with Nerissa, Portia claims that she will "speak of 'frays / Like a fine bragging youth; and tell quaint lies / How honorable ladies sought my love" (3.4.68-70). Whereas early modern notions of female virtue were based on chastity, silence, and obedience, Portia cherishes the opportunity to "brag," the opposite of the silence she would embody as wife. Her desire to "tell quaint lies, / How honorable ladies sought my love" does not reveal a homoerotic desire to have ladies seek her love, but instead points to Portia's desire for agency over her own body, to "choose" and "refuse" her own sexual partner.

When Nerissa asks, "Why, shall we turn to men?", Portia chides her with: "Fie, what a question's that, / If thou wert near a lewd interpreter!" (3.4.78-80). Like Antonio's "Fie! Fie!", Portia's "Fie" is an exclamation of both deflection and assent. She does not explicitly confirm or deny her desire to "turn to men" because that would render her unchaste and un-silent by the "lewd interpreters" of public opinion. By mirroring Portia and Antonio's terms of deflection, Shakespeare negotiates between desire and the limits imposed by a socially constructed reality.

Portia's desire for intellectual betterment is manifest in the letter she has Doctor Bellario send to the court. Writing herself into the male privilege that she cannot enjoy as a woman, the letter says:

> …we turned o'er many books together; he is furnished with my opinion which, bettered with his own learning, the greatness whereof I cannot enough commend, comes with him at my importunity, to fill up your grace's request in my stead. (4.1.154-8)

By crediting the learning of her male alter ego, Portia builds the fantasy of a masculine self that has the privilege of being "lessoned" by reading "many books." Specifying that the doctor's legal repertoire only *adds* to "his own learning," she implies that Balthazar's intellect has always existed within her. Portia proves this intellectual potential through her entrapment of Shylock:

> For it appears by manifest proceeding
> That indirectly, and directly too,
> Thou hast contrived against the very life
> Of the defendant (4.1.354-7)

Indeed, she demonstrates a convincing knowledge of the law, despite the intellectual limits imposed on her sex by gendered social norms. Her use of legal jargon shows that she genuinely has read legal books, books that were presumably available in the home library of her gentleman father. Although she lamented that her body was "aweary," it is clear that Portia has long been strengthening her mind.

By disguising herself as a man, Portia is able to pursue a more authentic side of herself. It is evident that her desire is fulfilled when she triumphs over what her male self can accomplish. Her joy is so strong that she refuses gifts in return for her legal victory, telling the unassuming Antonio and Bassanio:

> He is well paid that is well satisfied;
> And I delivering you am satisfied
> And therein do account myself well paid;
> My mind was never yet more mercenary. (4.1.411-4)

Portia declares her mind "mercenary" for intellectual freedom, much unlike her husband's financial motivations in Act 1. Her proud "I am satisfied" as Balthazar offers a conspicuous shift from Portia's openly dissatisfied opening lines: "My little body is aweary of this great world." This shift from a "weary" body to a mind that is "satisfied" indicates that Portia enjoys intellectual satisfaction as rewarding in and of itself. Finally able to pursue her own version of freedom, Shakespeare represents Portia's public victory as more fulfilling than the private victory of potentially conceiving a child on her wedding night.

The influence of Portia's masculine self is strong: her pride in fulfilling her own desires remains when she resumes her feminine role. Admonishing Bassanio for giving away her ring, she demonstrates a self-possession that contrasts with her self-deprecation of Act 3. Portia tells her husband:

> If you had known the virtue of the ring,
> Or half her worthiness that gave the ring,
> Or your own honour to contain the ring,
> You would not then have parted with the ring. (5.1.199-203)

At the beginning of the play, Bassanio suggested that the "wide world" was not "ignorant of her worth" (1.1.166); her eager male suitors, symbolic of the patriarchal social order, comprise this public opinion. Portia's rebuke of Bassanio shows how her cross-dressing experience allows her to recognize rather than repress her own self-value. After assuming masculinity through the public performance of her intellect, Portia develops a newfound determination to defend her value as a woman who deserves to be treated with respect, regardless of whether her husband desires her sexually.

Portia is not fighting for Bassanio's exclusive affection because she recognizes his interior bond with Antonio. In the courtroom, the men make their bond even more apparent, spurning discretion in their ignorance of Portia's presence. In this moment of dramatic emotional intensity, Bassanio declares his love for Antonio:

> I am married to a wife
> Which is as dear to me as life itself;
> But life itself, my wife, and all the world,
> Are not with me esteemed above thy life.
> I would lose all, ay, sacrifice them all
> Here to this devil, to deliver you. (4.1.278-83)

By telling the court that his wife's life is worth less to him than Antonio's, Bassanio publicly privileges his interior bond with Antonio over futurity with Portia. He implies that the sacrifice of his friend is too high an emotional cost to be worth the financial rewards of pledging himself eternally to a woman that can settle his debts. Bassanio refuses to privilege Edelman's "figural Child" over the demands of the present, which he strives to resolve by "hazarding all he has." In offering "all the world" in sacrifice to Shylock, Bassanio rhetorically attempts to compensate for Antonio's "hazarding" of his own risky fortunes. Antonio's empty purse defaulted him of his loan: he is the "tainted wether of the flock" (4.1.114) that is saved by the "potent ram." This potency, however, is located in Bassanio's marriage bond with the "fulsome ewe," Portia.

Bassanio's heated decree pledges to protect his bond with Antonio, showing that his chief desire is for an indefinite union with his friend, at both the figurative and literal expense of his marriage with Portia.

If the courtroom scene represents Bassanio's proposal to Antonio, their subsequent moments together symbolize an exchange of wedding vows, vows that threaten Bassanio's bond with Portia. Antonio convinces Bassanio to relinquish Portia's ring in order to physically represent his vow to sacrifice "life itself, my wife, and all the world" in return for Antonio's rescue. He tests Bassanio's devotion, saying: "My Lord Bassanio, let him have the ring. / Let his deservings and my love withal / Be valued 'gainst your wife's commandment" (4.1.445-7). Bassanio gives Balthazar the ring to demonstrate his ongoing commitment to Antonio, symbolically relinquishing his claim to his wife's womb in favor of his bond with Antonio. Antonio's "purse" may not reproduce, but Bassanio demonstrates his choice of the "purse" over the "ring," even while acknowledging his wife's "vantage to exclaim" on him.

Portia's "exclamation" begins as a threat of her own infidelity if her husband compromises her virtue. Yet, when she declares, "I will become as liberal as you" (5.1.226), her claim is more complex than a vexed wife's threat of cuckoldry. Lisa Jardine states that Shakespeare's cross-dressing heroines "mobilize a set of expectations of "knowingness," of sexual unruliness and ungovernability."[16] They negotiate between their desire to learn and a competing fear for their virtue. Portia threatens this "ungovernability" by implying her own sexual liaison with the Doctor. She tells Bassanio: "I'll not deny him anything I have, / No, not my body, nor my husband's bed: / Know him I shall, I am well sure of it" (5.1.227-9). In these lines, she renders her husband complicit in threatening her virtue; by giving away her ring, it is he who moves Portia to pursue extra-marital relations before even consummating their own marriage bond. Moreover, in threatening infidelity, Portia threatens the future of their "figural Child," now no longer the heir of their fortunes, but a potentially illegitimate child begotten as a result of Bassanio's own infidelity. In this way, Portia uses her intellect to negotiate the marriage's power dynamic in her own favor. However, the "vantage to exclaim" she desires from exposing her husband is not the opportunity to sleep with another man, but the right to pursue her own intellectual "liberality" as the Doctor. By catching Bassanio being unchaste, she reduces her own risk of being shamed for cross-dressing. Through her threat of exposure, Portia negotiates a means of excusing her own unruliness while demanding that her husband be more mindful of his marital responsibilities, despite being bound to Antonio.

Portia and Bassanio's mutual ungovernability renders their initial marriage bond a near-failure. The inability to abide by emerging social customs is what drives them to pursue desires outside of the marriage bond. Although the winner of the casket test was determined by who would "give and hazard all he hath" (2.9.20) in return for a woman who "stand[s] for sacrifice" (3.2.57), Portia and Bassanio each prove themselves unwilling to sacrifice the socially unacceptable desires that represent their most authentic selves. In this moment of greatest threat to the marriage bond, it is Antonio who offers to hazard himself. In offering to "be bound again" (5.1.251), he acknowledges the marriage bond's instability as resulting from his influence.

Instead of extending Bassanio's ungovernability, however, Antonio assigns himself the responsibility of limiting his extramarital impulses. When Antonio assures Portia that "I dare to be bound again, / My soul upon the forfeit, that your lord / Will nevermore break faith advisedly" (5.1.251-3), he binds himself to always be close to Bassanio in order to "advise" him on matters of fidelity. Antonio's proposed proximity negotiates a solution that perpetuates his interior bond with Bassanio, the cure to his original sadness, while ensuring that the marriage is consummated and the lines of futurity continue. Whereas Antonio had once threatened the marriage, he now renders his participation necessary to the strength of this union. When Antonio gives Bassanio Portia's ring and demands that he "swear to keep this" (5.1.256), Shakespeare uses irony not to depict a mode of accommodating homosexuality within the stifling emergence of heteronormativity, but rather, an accommodation of a heterosexual bond in the face of a desire that, far from not speaking its name, is "the love that won't shut up."[17]

Despite the common aim of performing a "queered" reading "against the grain" of *The Merchant of Venice*'s romance structure, my reading of the final marriage bond ultimately rejects Sinfield's claim that "the erotic potential of same-sex love is allowed a certain scope, but has to be set aside."[18] I disagree because Bassanio does not reject Antonio. They resolve that as long as Bassanio is married to Portia, Antonio will be by his side to "advise" him on how to keep "faith," renegotiating the terms of their interior bond to accommodate the conjugal bond. My reading provides a wholly different result from Sinfield's: the same-sex love is not set aside, but is a vital component of the new bond that contains the potential to render Portia and Bassanio's marriage bond all the stronger.

Bassanio's satisfaction with the new bond is evident. Upon learning of Portia's successful cross-dressing, he does not admonish her, but speaks flirtatiously: "Sweet doctor, you shall be my bedfellow; / When I am absent, then lie with my wife" (5.1.284-5). This mention of "absence" suggests Bassanio's intention to continue leaving Portia to pursue a form of sexual intimacy that she cannot deliver. Nonetheless, he also welcomes the Doctor, the cross-dressed Portia, as his own "bedfellow." Indeed, his enthusiasm upon Portia's declaration of her role as the doctor suggests that her mode of gender identification is an attraction that improves their sexual compatibility and the hope of a happier marriage. Portia assents to her husband's declared "absence," moments after their reunion because this agreement allows her to continue "lying" about her sex in order to pursue intellectual activities outside of patriarchal gender restrictions. In allowing her husband to "be absent," Portia herself can "lie with" the doctor. Through this resolution, Shakespeare negotiates an affective nexus in which a female character's story is resolved in her pursuit of her most authentic self. In doing so, she finally captures the continued sexual attention of her errant romance hero.

In this final exchange of vows, Antonio, Bassanio, and Portia, who had each been responsible for the original bond's near-failure, are now mutually responsible for the fulfillment of the renewed marriage bond. Rather than compete with each other, Portia and Antonio rely on each other. If Portia wants to pursue her masculine side, then her husband must "be absent"; for her husband to "be absent," Antonio must be present to ensure that Bassanio does not "break faith advisedly." Portia does not reject

Antonio because she needs Bassanio's desire for Antonio in order to pursue her most authentic self. Far from being a "third wheel," Antonio's role as the third member of the marriage bond is to stabilize what had once been a precarious balancing act. In this comic resolution, it is not these "alternate forms of relationality" that threaten marriage. Rather, it is marriage as an exclusively patriarchal and forcibly heteronormative form that tests the viability of Portia and Bassanio's nearly unconjugated marriage bond. *The Merchant of Venice* does not enforce a renunciation of alternate forms of relationality, but instead encourages a negotiation with them, a way to recognize the value of past paradigms while challenging the social function of new ones.

Notes

1. This argument originated in: Erin Weinberg, "'For when did friendship take/ A breed for barren metal of his friend?': Staging Love as Sterile Currency in *The Merchant of Venice*," presented at the *Poculi Ludique Societas* "Love, Sex and Romance in Early Drama" symposium at the University of Toronto, Toronto, Canada. (April 26, 2014).
2. Valerie Traub, *Desire and Anxiety: Circulations of Sexuality in Shakespearean Drama* (New York: Routledge, 1992), p. 146.
3. James M. Bromley, *Intimacy and Sexuality in the Age of Shakespeare* (Cambridge: Cambridge University Press, 2012), p. 2.
4. Alan Sinfield, *Shakespeare, Authority, Sexuality; Unfinished Business in Cultural Materialism* (London: Routledge, 2006), p. 20. "Queering the text" is a term that I borrow from Sinfield's lexicon.
5. Sinfield, *Shakespeare, Authority, Sexuality*, p. 20. Sinfield makes the important point that "it may be a mistake to regard the grain (always) as a property of the text." He suggests that the grain is the paradigm through which we read today, or, what he calls the "*the hegemonic critical condition*" (his italics).
6. See Gail Kern Paster, *Humoring the Body: Emotions and the Shakespearean Stage* (Chicago: Chicago University Press, 2004) and Gail Kern Paster, Katherine Rowe, and Mary Floyd-Wilson, eds., *Reading the Early Modern Emotions: Essays in the Cultural History of Emotions* (Philadelphia: University of Pennsylvania Press, 2004).
7. William Shakespeare. *The Merchant of Venice*, ed. M. M. Mahood. Updated Edition. (Cambridge: Cambridge University Press, 2003). All references are to this edition.
8. "purse, n., def. 7a". *OED Online*. December 2014. Oxford University Press. http://www.oed.com. (Accessed November 10, 2014).
9. Traub, *Desire and Anxiety*, pp. 6-7.
10. Lee Edelman, *No Future: Queer Theory and the Death Drive* (Durham and London: Duke University Press, 2004), p. 11.
11. "governor, n., def. 6" *OED Online*. March 2015. Oxford University Press. http://www.oed.com. (Accessed May 7, 2015).
12. Marc Shell, "'The Weather and the Ewe': Verbal Usury in *The Merchant of Venice*," *Kenyon Review* 1.4 (1979): 65-92, at p. 74.
13. Corinne S. Abate, "Nerissa teaches me what to believe": Portia's Wifely Empowerment in *The Merchant of Venice*," in *The Merchant of Venice: New Critical Essays*, ed. John W. Mahon and Ellen MacLeod (New York: Routledge, 2002), pp. 284-304 at p. 291.
14. Bromley, *Intimacy and Sexuality*, p. 10.
15. Alan Sinfield, "How to Read *The Merchant of Venice* Without Being Heterosexist," in *New Casebooks: The Merchant of Venice*, ed. Martin Coyle (New York: St. Martin's Press, 1998), pp. 161-80 at p. 164.
16. Lisa Jardine, "Cultural Confusion and Shakespeare's Learned Heroines: 'These are old paradoxes,'" *Shakespeare Quarterly* 38.1 (1987): 1-18 at p. 16.
17. Sinfield, "How to Read," 167.

18. Sinfield, "How to Read," 174.

"Most excellent warriers, very valiaunt": Reading Amazons in *A Midsummer Night's Dream* and *The Two Noble Kinsmen*

Kirsten Inglis

> These Amazones were most excellent warriers, very valiaunt, and without man's aduice did conquer mighty Countreyes, famous Cities, and notable Kingdomes, continuinge of longe time in one Seigniory and gouernment.
>
> ...
>
> If they were deliuered of males, ... they murdered them, or else brake their armes and legs in sutch wise as they had no power to beare weapons, and serued for nothynge else but to spin, twist, and to doe other feminine labour.
>
> - Painter, *The Palace of Pleasure*[1]

J begin with William Painter's characterization of Amazon women in *The Palace of Pleasure* (1567) because his articulation of the valour and the danger inherent in these figures exposes the deep ambivalence of Elizabethan attitudes towards the figure of the Amazon. On one hand, the Amazon represented an unruly and undomesticated woman who could and did live without men and who was as such a threat to the "natural" patriarchal order. In fact, as the second quotation from Painter makes apparent, it was a commonly held belief that Amazons either killed their men or forced them into feminine servility, wearing women's clothing and performing women's work.[2] On the other hand, Amazons were also cited by the Elizabethans as examples of bravery and martial prowess – attributes to be admired even in women. That their martial exploits culminated in a stable and long-lived government was also praised by Renaissance thinkers and perhaps reflected both anxieties over and hopes for Elizabeth I's reign. Printed nine years after Elizabeth took the throne, Painter's second tome begins with a description of "a straunge or miraculous port [sic. sort], (to our present skill) of womens gouernment...what combats and conflicts they durst attempt contrary to the nature of that sexe."[3] Despite Celeste Turner Wright's claim that "I have never found any Elizabethan comparing the Queen directly to an Amazon,"[4] this very comparison seems to be present in Painter's mind when he remarks to the book's dedicatee, George Howard, that "when her Maiestye's aduersary shal be readye to molest, she shal be prest (by God's assistance) to defend and march."[5] Again, Painter exposes Elizabethan notions of warlike women, deeming it fitting that Elizabeth march to war, but only when she is forced to do so. Painter clearly states that Elizabeth ("she") will "defend and march," although the reader likely understands this as figurative, a synecdoche in which the monarch stands in for the army of which she is head and does not literally lead the martial exploit. The image exposes and complicates expectations about the role of the monarch in warfare by drawing attention to Elizabeth's gender through feminine pronouns while simultaneously making explicit her presence on the battlefield; Painter thus invokes the idea of the Amazon without "comparing the Queen directly to an Amazon." Additionally, it is only with God's assistance that Elizabeth will (and should) lead her troops in martial defence. This short and seemingly simple statement of the Queen's role in warfare speaks to a new desire to understand and justify the role of women in martial exploits, a concern with which a plethora of treatises, dramas, and fictions about Amazons in the Elizabethan and early Jacobean period engaged.[6]

Among these representations, Shakespeare's *Midsummer Night's Dream* (1595-6) and Fletcher and Shakespeare's collaborative *Two Noble Kinsmen* (1613-4) are remarkable examples of a changing conception of both the Amazonian figure as symbol and of the shifting conception of women's roles both inside and outside the home. These two romances treat a common subtext – the marriage of Hippolyta and Theseus – and *Two Noble Kinsmen* is an adaptation of Chaucer's "Knight's Tale" (mid-1380s), itself an adaptation of Boccaccio's *Teseida* (1340-2). A consideration of the processes of adaptation in these works reveals the diverse symbolic programs and cultural concerns of authors translating the romance from page to stage. Even the two Renaissance plays evince different attitudes towards their Amazonian figures, with the later play providing a much more definitive silencing of Hippolyta and Emilia than does *A Midsummer Night's Dream*.[7] In taking up the figure of the Amazon in these texts, I argue that the "period when women began to enjoy some measure of freedom"[8] is the period in which there was the most interest in staging and, more importantly, in silencing the figure of the Amazon.

Earlier representations like Boccaccio's *Teseida* could and did depict a strong and vocal Amazonian figure precisely because this figure presented no overt threat to the patriarchal order from within which their authors were writing; likewise, the Chaucerian incarnation of the tale (with characteristic irony) reminds readers that the Amazon was not a figure likely to be easily silenced. Even the earlier Shakespeare play, *A Midsummer Night's Dream*, allows its Amazonian figure a measure of authority and agency within the confines of the marriage relationship. By the seventeenth century, however, there was real concern over the degradation of traditional roles for both men and women that led to a much more pressing desire to silence the figure of the Amazon and to rewrite her back into "safe" patriarchal social structures. Fueling the concern over gender roles in the period were such factors as travel narratives claiming to have discovered "real" Amazons in the New World, the return to the throne of a male monarch (James I) whose masculinity was itself called into question, and the spectacle of London women dressed as men in public.[9] David Cressy characterizes this latter phenomenon as "a challenge to patriarchal values, a bold assault on oppressive cultural boundaries" and Meg Lota Brown argues with reference to the early seventeenth-century transvestite controversy that these women, "simply by altering the fashion of their clothes…threatened the political distinctions that were at the heart of early modern social structures."[10] The controversy over women dressed as men in seventeenth-century London makes clear the growing concern with constraining and dictating women's movement and behaviour in the period. A woman who was not easily identifiable as a woman by her dress or manner posed a threat to social structures because in such garb it was conceivable that she would be treated as a man, an untenable notion for a society based on hierarchies in which women were "taught to cultivate the virtues of passivity and modesty, not the skills to govern, teach, or conduct business."[11] *The Two Noble Kinsmen*, far from subverting the patriarchal order by voicing and staging an independent, militant woman who desires to remain unwed, in fact reinforces patriarchal models of thought by silencing first Hippolyta and then Emilia in a much more decisive manner than either its source ("The Knight's Tale" / *Teseida*) or *A Midsummer Night's Dream* do.

Boccaccio's *Teseida* tells the story of Theseus' combat with the Amazon Hippolyta, her surrender to him, and the story of Arcites' and Palaemon's conflict over Hippolyta's sister Emilia. One of the striking elements of Boccaccio's poem is its narration of the bloody battle between Hippolyta and Theseus. Boccaccio's Hippolyta displays 'kingly' attributes that make her a good ruler. When she learns of Theseus' proposed attack, she is incensed, but instead of behaving rashly, she seeks "utile consiglio" [prudent council] (1.22) and addresses her people publicly, telling them that:

> l'gran Teseo di venir s'argomenta
> sopra di noi, avendoci moleste
> perché nostro piacer non si contenta
> di quell che l'atre, ciò è suggiacere
> a gli uomini, faccendo il lor volere. (1.26)[12]

[Theseus is planning to attack us, deeming us troublesome because we are not satisfied with remaining subject to men and obedient to their whims like other women.]

Hippolyta's awareness of the 'trouble' Amazons cause men articulates the very problem with Amazonian figures that the later adaptations of the tale pass over in silence. Boccaccio's Hippolyta is above all a prudent and brave leader, anticipating Theseus' attack, taking measures to arm her people, and patrolling every corner of her kingdom. When the battle commences, Theseus' men are confronted by *genti…avvallare / bene a cavallo armati*, "well-armed troops mounted on horses", who descend to the shore where the Greeks are anchored and prevent them from leaving their ships (1.47). It is significant that the Amazons' horsemanship is so strongly emphasized in this initial encounter with Theseus, with the narrator remarking that the women *in su cava' forti e isnelli / givano… (e que' correan come volano uccelli)*, "rode about on their strong, nimble horses… (which ran the way birds fly)]," since eventually both Palaemon and Arcites are defeated by horses – Palaemon by a flesh-eating Thracian horse in battle, and Arcites by the very horse upon which he celebrates his victory (1.70).[13] The strong association between the Amazons and their horses here emphasizes their rational and martial prowess; as Jeanne Addison Roberts argues, "skilful horsemanship is an image of success in war and of the individual's ability to control passion by reason."[14] In *Teseida* the Amazons are unequivocally associated with horses and horsemanship, like Theseus, like Palaemon and Arcites, and like the knights who later fight with Palaemon and Arcites to win Emilia, a fact that establishes them as virtuous warriors despite their eventual surrender to Theseus.

Unlike the later adaptations of the story, *Teseida* depicts Hippolyta's valour and bravery even after her submission to Theseus. This is not to say, however, that Boccaccio does not describe the Amazons' surrender in suggestive and submissive terms. In fact, he explicitly returns the women to their "natural" attire:

> Le donne avevan cambiati sembianti,
> ponendo in terra l'arme rugginose,
> e tornate eran quail eran davanti,
> belle, leggiadre, fresche e grazïose;
> e ora in lieti motti e dolci canti
> mutate avian le voci rigogliose,
> e' passi avevan piccioli tornati,
> che pria nell'armi grandi erano stati.
>
> [The ladies had altered their appearance as they placed their weapons on the ground and returned to the way they used to be: beautiful, charming, fresh, and graceful. Now with blithe movements and sweet songs they transformed their hearty voices; and their steps, which had been great strides before when they were bearing arms, became small again. (1.132)]

As the pamphlets of the seventeenth-century transvestite controversy also make clear, women's attire and demeanour are an essential part of their femininity. Before Theseus' men can woo and wed these women, they have to *look* like women. The return of the Amazons to feminine women is made both explicit and troubling in the *Teseida*, since even after her return to femininity and her submission to Theseus, Hippolyta remains unambiguously a warrior woman and clearly identifies herself as such. She even offers to fight on behalf of the Theban women herself, telling Theseus

> ben ch'io sia Amazòna,
> io non sí crudel, ch'a cota' cose
> volentier non mettessi la persona
> per vendicarle, sí son dispettose,
> se vero è ciò che delle donne sona
> il tristo ragionar

[although I am an Amazon, I am not so cruel that I would not willingly offer myself to avenge these wrongs, for they are so despicable, if the sad recital of these ladies is true. (2.41)]

Interestingly, it is the prudent Hippolyta who qualifies her acceptance of the Theban women's story by stressing that *if* their recital is true she would be willing to avenge them. Valour, bravery and reason coexist in a submissive, obedient, and feminine frame in Boccaccio's Hippolyta, something that later versions work to diminish. This coexistence, however, suggests that Hippolyta may not always be the submissive wife that Theseus desires, as she continues to define herself as an Amazon and even *arme portarvi disiava*, "wanted to bear arms," during the tournament of Palaemon and Arcites (8.93).

Both Hippolyta and Emilia remain dangerous to the social structure of Athens even after they are subsumed into the patriarchal order. As Arcites tells Palaemon in the glade, Theseus has *piú alta intenza*, "higher intentions," for Emilia than to give her in marriage to either of them (5.50). Emilia is destined for marriage to Achates, according to Theseus' will. Emilia, however, threatens to destabilize this prerogative through her ability to recognize and manipulate masculine desire. When Arcites and Palaemon first see Emilia in the garden Palaemon lets out an involuntary cry of love, which Emilia, despite her youth,

> intese…e parendole ciò saper per vero
> d'esser piaciuta seco si diletta,
> e piú se ne tien bella, e piú s'adorna
> qualora poi a quell giardin ritorna
> [understood,…took pleasure in, and considered herself even more beautiful, and now adorned herself the more every time she returned to the garden. (3.19)]

Emilia recognizes the two knights' desire and chooses to return to the garden dressed more alluringly each time she goes; she does not desire either of the men, as she wants to remain unwed, but she desires to see her own beauty reflected in their gaze.[15] Carla Freccero argues that the dominant strategy in the *Teseida* is one of containment, with Theseus' will triumphing over the resistance of the female figures throughout the book. She admits, however, that "there lingers a "remainder," the metaphorical consequence of the anxieties attendant upon such a process of courtly domestication."[16] Given the continuous reminders of Hippolyta's Amazonian past and Emilia's desire to remain unwed, I would argue that this remainder is more pronounced than Freccero credits. The Amazon figures in the *Teseida* are imperfectly contained and remain dangerous to Theseus' state even after their formal surrender (in battle and in marriage) to the patriarchal order.

This "remainder" of subversion and danger initially appears to be completely elided in Chaucer's version of the tale. It is somewhat surprising in light of the rollicking prologue and tale told by the Wife of Bath that Chaucer does not make more of the Amazonian figures of Hippolyta and Emilia in his version of the story in the "Knight's

Tale." As Suzanne Hagedorn notes, however, the tale as told by the Knight reflects this character's desire "to preserve the male power structures of chivalry" within which he himself is implicated.[17] In fact, the Knight is explicitly characterized as "a worthy man" who "loved chivalrie, / Trouthe and honour, fredom and curteisie" (General Prologue 43, 45-46).[18] The Knight's listeners certainly seem to believe this characterization of him, though Chaucer's reader may take a more cynical view of this portrayal, especially given the dubious nature of some of the military campaigns with which the Knight has been involved.[19] He is (or at least he believes he is) the perfect pattern of chivalric knighthood, and in order to uphold the social structures that sustain him, the Knight must "limit the disruptive potential of women, by shutting them up and shutting them (and their stories) out".[20] The subject of the first book of the *Teseida* is condensed and recounted by the Knight as:

> Ther was a duc that highte Theseus;...
> with his wysdom and his chivalrie,
> He conquered al the regne of Femenye...
> And weddede the queene Ypolita,
> And broghte hire hoom with hym in his contree
> With muchel glorie and greet solempnytee,
> And eek hir yonge suster Emelye. (860-71)

The Knight does note that if he had time he would tell the whole story of the siege of Ypolita and her marriage to Theseus, although he does not hint that this tale would be anything more than an encomium to "Theseus and ... his chivalrye" (878). As it is, he says, "the remenant of the tale is long ynough" (888). While this may seem like a thoughtful gesture on the Knight's part (he is solicitous of his audience's attention span and cognizant of the need for "every felawe [to] telle his tale" in a timely manner (890)), it is inescapable that whenever he chooses to leave something out of the story, it invariably seems to be an aspect of the original tale that could be construed as subversive or troubling.

As readers of the often cheeky Chaucer, we grow alert to the text's cues and clues that there may indeed be more to the story. There is, for example, no mention of Ypolita and Emelye's reactions to the Theban women's pleas to Theseus, as there is in *Teseida*. Instead, the narrator says, Theseus

> ...sente anon Ypolita the queene,
> And Emelye, hir yonge suster sheene,
> Unto the toun of Atthenes to dwelle,
> And forth he rit; *ther is namoore to telle*. (971-974, italics mine)

Again, we are made aware that there is something missing from this tale, although perversely, the Knight reveals this by claiming there is nothing missing from his tale. Throughout *The Canterbury Tales*, however, such moments become increasingly obvious as moments where the aims of the tale-teller (here the Knight) and the author-as-narrator are discernibly different. The Knight wants his listeners to hear and believe that his tale is the definitive version of the story, while Chaucer asks his readers to recognize a story with a historical and literary precedent and to consider what is being left out.

In the "The Knight's Tale," what is left out is often that which could prove subversive or destabilizing to a patriarchal, chivalric social system. In *Teseida* Emilia, though innocent, nevertheless understands that she is the object of Palaemon and Arcites' affection, and she encourages this by purposefully adorning herself on her visits to the garden;[21] in "The Knight's Tale," on the other hand, there is no suggestion that Emelye knows what the knights feel for her. She is utterly silent and without agency in the garden as she "gadereth floures, party white and rede, / To make a subtil gerland for hire hede" (1053-4). Emelye could not be further from an image of Amazonian martial prowess here, and the knights' first sighting of her is described solely in terms of their reaction to her. After their initial sighting of Emelye, the two do not look on her again; they describe her to each other and recount their own perceptions of the woman. The scene becomes an argument over the relative right that each knight has to claim Emelye, and the two rely on a discourse of chivalric love in order to stake their claims.

The Knight himself participates in this discourse of chivalric love by posing a *question d'amour* to his listeners. Which of the knights, he asks his fellow pilgrims when Arcite is released but exiled and Palamon remains in prison but able to see Emelye, "hath the worse, Arcite or Palamoun?" (1348). The Knight's question serves to focus the reader's attention solely on the two men, and Emelye all but disappears from the tale at this point. Rather than reading this as Chaucer's deliberate silencing of the female figures in the text (especially given his vocalization of women in other texts), I read this focus on the two men as a narrative technique that is perfectly appropriate in the character of the Knight. The Knight is still very much vested in the chivalric code: he is accorded a place of honour among the other pilgrims, he is training his son (the Squire) as a knight, he has fought in numerous foreign campaigns and distinguished himself, and it should come as no surprise that what interests him in his own tale are the chivalric exploits of other knights, not the potentially shameful spectacle of martial women.[22] In the Knight's tale it is he who writes Ypolita and Emelye back into the patriarchal order through Theseus, who physically takes Emelye's hand and gives it to Palamon, informing her she will wed him. In the context of the larger *Canterbury Tales*, the Knight succeeds in his story, since "in al the route nas ther yong ne oold / That he ne seyde it was a noble storie," and it is, we are told, especially the gentlefolk who find this tale compelling (3110-11).

For the Knight, then, shutting up and out the voices of the Amazons in his tale proves an appropriate and successful narrative strategy, at least as far as the internal audience of the tale is concerned. The external audience for the tale, Chaucer's reader, recognizing the somewhat dubious character of the Knight and perhaps remembering the Boccaccian precedent for the tale, likely took this "happy ending" with a pinch of salt. In fact the Knight's very insistence on the "blisse and melodye" (3097) in which the couple lives with "never…no word hem bitwene / Of jalousie or any oother teene" (3106) should alert the reader to another moment of elision or omission in the story. While the Knight's listeners applaud the chivalric happy ending, including the silencing of the Amazonian women, Chaucer's readers may not be expected to so wholeheartedly accept the Knight's version of events. Given the sardonic tone of Chaucer's work, the tale's silencing of its female characters and its insistence on Emelye's obedience in fact leaves the reader to question the Knight's interpretation of the tale's Amazons as willing and quiet subjects of masculine authority.

When Shakespeare takes up the narrative of Theseus and Hippolyta's wedding as a frame for *Midsummer Night's Dream* and, with John Fletcher, adapts the story of Arcite and Palamon in *The Two Noble Kinsmen*, the verse narratives of Boccaccio and Chaucer become dramatic representations, exposing new and different nuances of the tales.[23] *Midsummer Night's Dream*, written late in Elizabeth I's reign (the queen would have been in her sixties when it was produced), stages the events surrounding Theseus and Hippolyta's nuptials, namely the love plot of Hermia, Helena, Demetrius, and Lysander, the mechanicals' play, and the struggle between Oberon and Titania. Kathryn Schwarz argues that the spectacle of the Amazonian wife "synthesiz[es] a range of performances in a single body and demonstrat[es] that definitions shift."[24] *Midsummer Night's Dream* stages a female body in which the binaries of feminine/masculine, dominant/submissive, and ruler/subject converge and collapse, and offers, I argue, a powerful representation of Hippolyta as an Amazonian woman despite the fact that she is presented as a largely silent part of the framing device for the play. This is a representation that is possible and perhaps prudent near the end of Elizabeth I's reign, when collapsing femininity and martial power in a single body could be seen as praise for a "Virgin Queen" whose symbolic power relied on the image of marriage to her nation and the concept of the monarch's two bodies, specifically framed by Elizabeth as a way of reconciling the masculine/feminine binary in a single self. Shakespeare's play thus presents a more directly positive image of the Amazonian figure than does Chaucer's tale (relying as it does on irony and elision in order to recuperate the Knight's version of the Amazons). This representation changes once again in Shakespeare and Fletcher's *Two Noble Kinsmen*, when the return to the English throne of a male monarch and a conservative drive to restrict and repress gender roles give the staged body of a martial woman a much more troubling symbolism than in earlier narratives. In fact, I argue that in the later play Shakespeare and Fletcher introduce Hippolyta and Emilia as more potentially subversive (as in, for example, the play's greater focus on female homosocial bonds) than their counterparts in Boccaccio or Chaucer are; this is done precisely in order to emphasize more clearly their silencing and subjection to masculine power at the play's end.

The list of characters for *Midsummer Night's Dream* names Hippolyta as "Hippolyta, Queen of the Amazons, betrothed to Theseus."[25] In this play, the audience sees Hippolyta primarily in relation to her marriage – during the betrothal and immediately following her marriage – and her presence in the play at the moment of her legal subjection to Theseus on the one hand "validates the ordering principle that locates sexual authority in men,"[26] and on the other hand, locates a voice of dissent in the troubling body of an Amazon woman. Hippolyta shows no hesitation in speaking her mind, even when this puts her into direct conflict with her betrothed Theseus.[27] Additionally, given the explicit characterization in the *dramatis personae* of Hippolyta as an Amazon, it seems fair to assume that she would have been costumed in such a way as to remind the audience of her female sex and of the masculine-gendered acts (warfare, the slaughter of men) in which she had been implicated. The audience is also told at the outset of the play that Theseus "wooed thee with my sword, / And won thy love, doing thee injuries" (1.1.16-7), so that the violent nature of their courtship is made perfectly clear and remains the defining characteristic of their relationship. As Katherine Schwarz argues, "Hippolyta demonstrates that patriarchally governed heterosociality rests on fragile and fluid distinctions.... Her presence does not display suppression or repression or oppression already accomplished, but signals that these processes...are always ongoing and never complete."[28] The competitive strain in Theseus and Hippolyta's exchange in the woods is a case in point. Hippolyta recalls being with Hercules and Cadmus "when in a wood of Crete they bay'd the bear / With hounds of Sparta" (4.1.113-14) and Theseus responds as though challenged by a masculine rival. His response is immediate and its tone defensive:[29]

> My hounds are bred out of the Spartan kind;
> [...] A cry more tuneable
> Was never hollow'd to, nor cheered with horn,
> In Crete, in Sparta, nor in Thessaly.
> Judge when you hear. (4.1.119-26)

In this play, Theseus (unlike his counterpart in *Two Noble Kinsmen*) does not seem to desire his fiancée's complete subjection to his rule. In fact, while Theseus waits eagerly for the "nuptial hour" (1.1.1) that will literally subject Hippolyta to her husband, he continuously solicits her opinion and, in the competitive extract above, appears perfectly content to abide by Hippolyta's judgement of the "contest."

Nevertheless, Theseus realizes that his governance of Hippolyta is incomplete, and this suggests a tension between the couple that I argue is present even from the play's first scene. Theseus, after decreeing Hermia must submit to her father's will or face death or a convent, dismisses the various participants in the exchange (Demetrius, Egeus, and Hermia) but addresses Hippolyta with the gentle "Come, my Hippolyta; what cheer, my love?" (1.1.122). Of course, this line when delivered in performance could be given any number of expressions; it is the only question in the exchange, however, and even if rhetorical in nature, must contrast significantly with the autocratic, imperative statements issued to the other characters. The line embodies the tension in the relationship between Amazon and conqueror, since it twice reminds Hippolyta of her subject position ('*my* Hippolyta' and '*my* love') while nevertheless appearing to be an invitation issued by an equal rather than a command issued by a superior. Finally, while the phrase "what cheer" may be a standard greeting, it does question Hippolyta's mood or well-being and I wonder whether there is something in Hippolyta's countenance that prompts Theseus to use this particular phrase. Again, performances may choose to emphasize this moment differently, but I would suggest that Hippolyta is perhaps less than acquiescent to Theseus' ultimatum to Hermia. Hermia desires what Hippolyta herself is supposed to have had: the ability to choose her own marriage partner, rather than bowing to the dictates of a father or other (male) guardian.[30] In fact, Hermia's statement at 1.1.59 – "I know not by what power I am made bold" – could be played to emphasize Hippolyta's solidarity with her. Perhaps it is Hermia's love for Lysander that emboldens her, but perhaps Hippolyta's countenance communicates her support for Hermia's boldness. Hippolyta's character is rich in performative potential precisely because she is present but often silent.

A Midsummer Night's Dream, while not an adaptation of *Teseida* or "The Knight's Tale," is important in considering the development of the Amazonian figure in Shakespeare's work, representing as it does an Elizabethan version of the Amazon that is at odds with the characters as taken up more than a decade later in *The Two Noble Kinsmen*. Hippolyta and Theseus' wedding is a framing device for the larger plot of *A Midsummer Night's Dream*, a structural fact that means Hippolyta is not central to the narrative of the work. Nevertheless, Shakespeare does imbue her throughout with the laudable martial qualities that are present in Boccaccio's tale and ironically elided in Chaucer's. Her military prowess, autonomy, outspokenness and subversive performance potential are never fully subsumed to Theseus's authority and she thus remains a figure of resistance to patriarchal authority in a way that the Amazon figures of *The Two Noble Kinsmen* cannot. The changing political climate of the seventeenth century makes the spectre of masculine women (and, conversely, feminine men) an image that urgently needs to be contained, as Hippolyta and Emilia will most decisively be in Shakespeare and Fletcher's *The Two Noble Kinsmen*.

While the presentation of Theseus and Hippolyta in *A Midsummer Night's Dream* shows remarkable differences from their portrayal in *Two Noble Kinsmen*, there are also significant correspondences between the narrative their story frames and the story of Arcite and Palamon. Theseus' first act in *A Midsummer Night's Dream* is to articulate the patriarchal order in questions of marriage; "To you your father should be as a god" (1.1.47), he tells Hermia, and "your eyes must with his judgement look" (1.1.57). Hermia is given a stark ultimatum by Theseus, who in effect bestows her in marriage in the same arbitrary manner as he bestows Emilia in the earlier tales, casually threatening death as a means of restoring the patriarchal order. The love plot in which Demetrius and Lysander both fall for Helena reveals another parallel to the story of Arcite and Palamon: Schwarz argues that Demetrius and Lysander are "doubled in their erotic connection to a single woman, nearly indistinguishable in their language of love and violence,"[31] and the same could be said of Arcite and Palamon in Boccaccio's and Chaucer's earlier narratives as well as in *Two Noble Kinsmen*. These men become virtually indistinguishable from each other as the arbitrariness of their love for Helena or Emilia is made manifest.

The relationship that Emilia describes in *Two Noble Kinsmen* between herself and Flavina also parallels the childhood relationship between Hermia and Helena in *A Midsummer Night's Dream*. Just as Hermia and Helena were once "Two lovely berries molded on one stem; / So, with two seeming bodies, but one heart," (3.2.211-12), Emilia and Flavina once loved as one:

> but I
> And she I sigh and spoke of were things innocent,
> Loved for we did and like the elements
> That know not what nor why, yet do effect

Rare issues by their operance; our souls
Did so to one another. (1.3.59-64)[32]

A Midsummer Night's Dream, Schwarz claims, "moves away from homoerotic self-sufficiency" as Hermia and Helena are brought into the patriarchally sanctioned state of heterosexual marriage.[33] In the same way, *Two Noble Kinsmen* "moves away from homoerotic self-sufficiency" as the bond between Palamon and Arcite is severed by heterosexual love and death, and the bond between Flavina and Emilia is clearly already in the past. Emilia's description of her love for Flavina (prompted by the women's discussion of the bond of perfect friendship and love between Theseus and Pirithous) moves Hippolyta, but she is not, she says, "ripe for... persuasion" (1.3.91) away from Theseus. Nor, she believes, does Pirithous present a true rival for Theseus's affections; Hippolyta concludes that she "more than his Pirithous, possess[es] / The high throne in his heart" (1.3.95-6). The bond between Theseus and Pirithous, presented in *Teseida* and "The Knight's Tale" in quasi-legendary terms, is here confirmed to be a thing of the past as Theseus moves into a space of heterosexual union with Hippolyta. While the staging and voicing of the strength of homosocial bonds between women is something introduced in the Renaissance telling of the Amazonian narrative and would appear to challenge the primacy of the homosocial bonds between men (bonds which often cement or consolidate power), it is significant that both male and female homosocial bonds are ultimately written out of the plays in a reiteration of the importance and pre-eminence of the marriage relationship.

Emilia's image as sexually self-sufficient and without desire for marriage with anyone (least of all Arcite or Palamon) presents her as a greater potential threat to the patriarchal system than her counterparts in earlier versions of the tale. As Laurie Shannon argues:

> [Emilia] provides a fully developed articulation of an Amazonian position, situating herself affectively and socially among women alone. She not only connects chastity with a female associational preference; her idea of her reputation and her identity is drawn from and maintained within the company of women.[34]

Emilia's community of women has already, however, been eroded by the betrothal of Hippolyta and Theseus. Hippolyta in fact aligns herself with Theseus against Emilia's desires, her "You must go" distinctly echoing Theseus' "You must be there," as the two attempt to make Emilia watch the combat between Arcite and Palamon (5.3.28, 18). When they come across Arcite and Palamon fighting in the grove, Hippolyta commands Emilia to "Speak not to be denied" or "that face of yours / Will bear the curses else of after ages / For these lost cousins" (3.6.186-8). Hippolyta, now the kneeling subject of her lord Theseus, aids him in his subjection of Emilia to a marriage with an arbitrarily chosen suitor that Emilia claims repeatedly she does not desire; Hippolyta's participation in the imposition of marriage on Emilia makes her own subjugation to Theseus all the more apparent. This is a marked contrast to the reminders of her martial past in *Teseida*, the ironic silencing of her in "The Knight's

Tale," or her outspokenness and strength in *A Midsummer Night's Dream*. The later play is much more concerned with suppressing its martial women than earlier versions of the tale have been, a development that I argue is connected to the conservative cultural drive at work in the decade of the play's composition. Susan Wing contends that in *Two Noble Kinsmen* "Emilia's role is greatly expanded from Chaucer's passive, silent object of love, and she displays considerably more personality and psychological complexity than Boccaccio'."[35] I find it difficult, however, to credit the implication that this characterization is a sign of the playwrights' progressive thinking around the issue of women's rights. In fact, Shakespeare and Fletcher allow Emilia and Hippolyta to appear as more dangerous and subversive figures than Boccaccio and Chaucer do in order to silence them more definitively at the play's end. As in *Teseida* and *Midsummer Night's Dream*, Hippolyta is remembered as a valiant warrior; the Theban queens apply to her after Theseus turns away, invoking her as "Honoured Hippolyta, / Most dreaded Amazonian, that hast slain / The scythe-tusked boar" (1.1.77-9). What they ask of her, however, is not that she use her physical force on their behalf, as Hippolyta offers to do in the *Teseida*, but that she "speak't in woman's key; like such a woman / As any of us three; weep ere you fail" (1.1.94-5). Hippolyta is to use her womanly wiles, her supplication and her tears, to induce Theseus' aid on behalf of the Theban queens. The women's reminder of Hippolyta's subjection to Theseus is all the more powerful after their invocation of her former Amazonian might; they are the first (though not the last) in the play to repeat and reinforce the transformation from Amazon to kneeling wife.

    The other striking transformation is, of course, Emilia's shift at the play's end from self-sufficient martial maid to silent wife, as she is passed from man to man at Theseus' will. Emilia's subjection is made manifest in the language used to address her in the final act. Theseus commands her to "give me your hands" (5.3.109). Arcite tells her that "to buy you, I have lost what's dearest to me, save what is bought" (5.3.112-13). Arcite, on his death bed tells Palamon to "Take Emilia…Take her. I die" (5.4.90-5). And, finally, Theseus authorizes Emilia's transfer to Palamon, telling him to "Lead your lady off" (5.4.122). Emilia is reduced to chattel, led like a piece of horseflesh off-stage, recalling Arcite's dubious compliment to Emilia that "I purchase cheaply, / As I do rate your value" (5.3.113-14). Emilia could not be further from the proto-feminist position ascribed to her by Wing, and her silence and subjection are all the more conspicuous for her earlier verbal strength and the play's repeated reminders of her Amazonian past. This contrasts particularly with Chaucer's ironic presentation of the silenced Amazons, of whose agency the reader is repeatedly reminded by the insistence that "there is no more to tell," a device that urges the reader to challenge the ideal of the silent and subject wife. The audience of *Two Noble Kinsmen* is not challenged to critique its representation of Emilia. Instead, the audience seems to be encouraged to accept her subjugation. Her silent presence allows for the promise of a properly heterosexual union for Palamon and the opportunity for Theseus and the audience to reflect on the vagaries of fortune, presented by Theseus as the gods, the "heavenly charmers" (5.4.131), who play with the lives of mortal men.

    The significantly divergent portrayals of the Amazon figures in *Midsummer Night's Dream* and *Two Noble Kinsmen* reflect a distinct political shift over the period during which the plays were written. I would suggest that *Midsummer Night's Dream*'s representation of Hippolyta as an Amazonian figure who is implicitly and at times explicitly opposed to Theseus' vocalized commands is appropriate to a play written during Elizabeth I's reign. Although overt comparisons between the Queen and an Amazon were likely ill-advised – the Amazonian figure was, after all, a figure of ambiguous virtue in the Renaissance – the implication must surely have been present that a virgin ruler with the "heart and stomach of a king" in many ways resembled an Amazonian figure, so that a subtle portrayal could have the effect of invoking the authority of a queen whose "two bodies" allowed for the synthesis of martial power and femininity. Simon Shepherd has argued with regard to Amazon figures in Renaissance Italy that the willingness to represent Amazons without silencing them may have to do with the reality of female rulership.[36] It seems that the same can be said of Elizabethan England, as the image of Amazonian agency in *A Midsummer Night's Dream* is an acceptable and perhaps even flattering image in a state with a powerful and unwed woman as its political head. Less than twenty years later when *Two Noble Kinsmen* was written, however, James I was on England's throne; with him came a desire for the return to more conservative roles for both men and women.[37] Writing women back into the social order, restoring their femininity and validating masculine power and prowess is a far more pressing concern in the later play.

The specific changes introduced to the Amazon figures by each successive author reflect cultural shifts in thinking about the way in which women participated in society; from martial to marital expectations, from homosocial to heterosocial relationships, from matriarchal to patriarchal structures, the changes that Amazons undergo in these narratives reveal social ideals about the way in which feminine identity can or should be created against masculine images of power and desire. The image of Amazonian society is uncanny and unsettling as it distorts patriarchal hierarchies, and so the Amazon must be taken out of isolation; there can be no self-sufficient society of women who "treated maryage…with condition" that the men would assemble for breeding purposes only and then "returne home agayne to their own houses."[38] While each of these Amazonian stories treats the marriage of Hippolyta and Theseus and writes the Amazon back into patriarchal societal structures, they do so in subtly but remarkably different ways. Boccaccio's brave and prudent governor whose martial past is never fully in the past becomes, in Chaucer's tale, a silent wife whose silence the reader is led to question as well as a framing narrative for the story of chivalric competition, and the knowing and active Emilia of *Teseida* becomes the Knight's silent, beautiful prize. The two Renaissance plays appear to reclaim a measure of authority and agency for the Amazon women, presenting dramatically complex figures and allowing them to speak throughout. Paradoxically, however, it is the framing-figure of *Midsummer Night's Dream* who reflects the more subversive vision of the wedded Amazon as she asserts herself – reminders of her past and her present opinions – in her relationship with Theseus, while the figures of Hippolyta and Emilia are introduced in *Two Noble Kinsmen* as strong martial women only to be repeatedly and dramatically silenced by masculine desires and the properly patriarchal institution of marriage.

Notes

1. William Painter, "The Amazones," in *The Palace of Pleasure* Vol. II, ed. Joseph Jacobs (New York: Dover, 1966).

2. Spenser's Artegall is, for example, forced to wear women's clothing and spin when he is captured by the Amazon Radigund in Book V of *The Faerie Queene*. Britomart, the knight of chastity and a warrior woman who is definitively not an Amazon, is appalled when she rescues Artegall and "saw that lothly uncouth sight, / Of men disguiz'd in womanishe attire" (5.7.37). Britomart sets about restoring the natural order, "restoring / to mens subiection" (5.7.42) the Amazon women. Edmund Spenser, *The Faerie Queene*, ed. A.C. Hamilton (London: Longman, 2001).

3. Painter, "Amazones," p. 154.

4. Celeste Turner Wright, "The Amazons in Elizabethan Literature," *Studies in Philology* 37 (1940): 433-456 at p. 445.

5. Painter, "Amazones," pp. 152-3.

6. Apparently factual accounts include those of classical authors like Plutarch and Statius as well as more current treatises like Thevet's *New Found World* (trans. 1568), Raleigh's *History of the World* (1614), and Hakluyt's *Voyages* (1596). Literary representations in the Renaissance include: Ariosto's *Orlando Furioso* (1532), Painter's *Palace of Pleasure* (1575), Spenser's *Faerie Queene* (1596), Sidney's *Arcadia* (1590), Shakespeare's *Midsummer Night's Dream* (1596), Shakespeare and Fletcher's *Two Noble Kinsmen*, Fletcher's *Bonduca* (1610-14), and Fletcher and Massinger's *The Sea Voyage* (1662), among many others.

7. While some of the representational differences may be attributable to the collaborative nature of *Two Noble Kinsmen*, it is beyond the scope of this paper to enter into the debate over whether and to what extent Shakespeare was involved in the play. I argue that the play evinces a representational strategy that reflects to some extent a cultural *zeitgeist*, regardless of the precise nature of the collaboration. For discussions of the authorship question, see *Sources of Four Plays Ascribed to Shakespeare:* The Reign of King Edward III, Sir Thomas More, The History of Cardenio, The Two Noble Kinsmen, ed G. Harold Metz (Columbia: University of Missouri Press, 1989) and Lois Potter's introduction to The Arden Shakespeare *The Two Noble Kinsmen*, ed. Lois Potter (Walton-on-Thames: Thomas Nelson and Sons, 1997).

8. Wright, "Amazons," p. 433.

9. On the desire for a return to more traditional masculine and feminine roles in Jacobean England due in part to James I's own perceived effeminacy, see for example, Derek Hirst, *England in Conflict, 1603-1660: Kingdom, Community, Commonwealth* (London: Arnold, 1999).

10. David Cressy, "Gender Trouble and Cross-Dressing in Early Modern England," *Journal of British Studies* 35 (1996): 438-465, at p. 440. See also Meg Lota Brown and Kerri Boyd McBride, *Women's Roles in the Renaissance* (London: Greenwood, 2005), p. 126. Brown notes that women cross-dressed in the seventeenth-century for many and complex reasons, including "to avoid marriage and men's sexual advances…as a cover for a same-sex relationship…to ensure her own safety [when travelling]…to enter traditionally male occupations" (82).

11. Brown, *Women's Roles, p. 4*. By the early seventeenth century, when Shakespeare and Fletcher wrote *The Two Noble Kinsmen*, a host of social and cultural factors combined to create a perceived threat to established hierarchical social structures. These factors include a new, male,

monarch on the throne; concern over Scottish influence in the court; anxiety about a perceived weakening of traditional gender roles, particularly because of James I's own perceived effeminacy; and debate over the level of foreign military action in which England should be involved.

12. Giovanni Boccaccio, *Teseida delle nozze d'Emilia*, ed. Aurelio Roncaglia (Bari: Gius. Laterza & Figli, 1941). Translations are from Bernadette McCoy, *Teseida*, (New York: Medieval Text Association, 1974).

13. In *Two Noble Kinsmen*, Arcite is killed by a horse given to him by Emilia, emphasizing the disastrous consequences of a man who is unable to control his mount and, by association, his wife. On the equestrian symbolism of Arcite's death in *Two Noble Kinsmen*, see Paula S. Berggren, "'For What We Lack, / We Laugh': Incompletion and 'The Two Noble Kinsmen,'" *Modern Language Studies* 14 (1984): 3-17, at pp. 11-13.

14. Jeanne Addison Robertson, "Crises of Male Self-Definition in *The Two Noble Kinsmen*," in *Shakespeare, Fletcher, and* The Two Noble Kinsmen, ed. Charles H. Frey (Columbia: University of Missouri Press, 1989), pp. 133-144, at p. 143.

15. Emilia is also the only one who recognizes 'Pentheus' as Arcites when he reappears in Athens. She keeps quiet, however, enjoying his attentions, until he and Palamon fight each other in the woods.

16. Carla Freccero, "From Amazon to Court Lady: Generic Hybridization in Boccaccio's *Teseida*," *Comparative Literature Studies* 32 (1995): 226-243, at p. 230.

17. Suzanne C. Hagedorn, *Abandoned Women: Rewriting the Classics in Dante, Boccaccio, & Chaucer* (Ann Arbor: University of Michigan Press, 2004), p. 101.

18. Geoffrey Chaucer, *The Riverside Chaucer*, ed. Larry D. Benson (Oxford: Oxford University Press, 1987).

19. For some perspectives on the irony (or lack thereof) in the Knight's depiction, see for example, Jill Mann, *Chaucer and Medieval Estates Satire* (Cambridge: Cambridge University Press, 1973); Angela J. Weisl, *Conquering the Reign of Femeny: Gender and Genre in Chaucer's Romance* (Cambridge: Brewer, 1995); and Lee Patterson, *Chaucer and the Subject of History* (London: Routledge, 1991), especially Chapter 3, "*The Knight's Tale* and the Crisis of Chivalric Identity."

20. Hagedorn, *Abandoned Women*, p. 101.

21. Although this image of womanhood draws on a stereotype of women that depicts them as overwhelmingly vain, it does allow Emilia a perspective on the two lovers and ascribes to her a certain amount of agency in the lovers' pursuit of her.

22. This represents yet another moment where the reader is conscious of the rhetorically distinct positions of the tale-teller and the author. The Knight certainly takes himself seriously, as do the other pilgrims; the reader is conscious of the Knight's violent and pompous nature, and it suits Chaucer's satiric portrayal of the Knight to have him focus squarely on masculine chivalric valour in his tale to the exclusion of the Amazonian figures.

23. It would be interesting to consider the way in which Hippolyta and Emilia were staged in the Renaissance theatre. As Kathryn Schwarz argues, the figure of the Amazon makes sex "a public display" and the spectacle of self-mutilation (the removal of a breast that was commonly reported in source material) "frustrates expectations of eroticism and nurture" (*Tough Love: Amazon Encounters in the English Renaissance* (Durham, NC: Duke University Press, 2000),

pp. 4-5). Was the missing breast suggested in the Amazons' costuming, or would this destroy the characters' erotic potential? The extent to which Hippolyta is a submissive or subversive figure in modern performances of the play remains very much a function of directorial vision.

24. Schwarz, *Tough Love*, p. 20.

25. William Shakespeare, *A Midsummer Night's Dream*, ed. Roma Gill (Oxford: Oxford University Press, 2005).

26. Schwarz, *Tough Love*, p. 207

27. See for, example, 1.1.7-11, in which Hippolyta offers a resolute and reassuring speech to Theseus on their upcoming nuptials; 5.1.23-7, in which Hippolyta directly contradicts Theseus's dismissive reading of the lovers' tale; and 5.1.85 and following, in which Hippolyta and Theseus discuss the entertainment to be (and then being) offered.

28. Schwarz, *Tough Love*, p. 210.

29. Schwarz discusses the implications of this claim, patently untrue, since "Cadmus, founder of Thebes, precedes Hippolyta and Hercules by several mythological generations" (*Tough Love*, p. 213). Whether or not we read Hippolyta as telling a true story from her past or as appropriating a masculine history not her own, the tension this claim causes for Theseus is apparent.

30. Hippolyta is of course violently subdued by Theseus; however, in this play she is explicitly characterized as having been wooed (violently, but still wooed) and not disposed of by a patriarch, as Hermia is (by both father and ruler).

31. Schwarz, *Tough Love*, p. 212.

32. John Fletcher and William Shakespeare, *The Two Noble Kinsmen*, ed. Lois Potter (London: Arden, 2002).

33. Schwarz, *Tough Love*, p. 220.

34. Laurie J. Shannon, "Emilia's Argument: Friendship and 'Human Title' in *The Two Noble Kinsmen*," *ELH* 64 (1997): 657-682, at p. 671.

35. Susan L. Wing, "Something About Emilia: Woman as Love Object in Boccaccio, Chaucer, Anne de Graville, and Shakespeare and Fletcher," *Literary Studies East and West* 1 (1989): 139-151, at p. 146.

36. Simon Shepherd, *Amazons and Warrior Women: Varieties of Feminism in Seventeenth-Century Drama* (New York: St. Martin's, 1981), p. 6.

37. This is an issue taken up by the anonymous pamphlets *Hic Mulier* and *Haec Vir* only a few years later; for example, Anon, *Haec Vir, or The Womanish Man*, in *Half Humankind*, ed. Katherine Usher Henderson and Barbara F. McManus (Urbana: University of Illinois Press, 1985), pp. 278-9. The pamphlets take the form of a dialogue, with *Hic Mulier* (the mannish-woman) discoursing with *Haec Vir* (the womanish-man). While the speakers each perform a gendered role, there is not enough evidence to connect a biologically male or female author with the pamphlets. *Haec Vir*, for example, appears to make a resounding declaration of women's equality with the assertion that women "are as freeborn as Men, have as free election and as free spirits"; however, this position develops as a rhetorical pose, a role performed in order to arouse disgust and outrage in readers in preparation for the coming denunciation of the perversity of male effeminacy (284). By establishing both rhetorical skill and the perversity of female cross-dressing in the initial stages of the dialogue, *Hic Mulier* prepares her readers to accept the logic of her

final argument and her exhortation to men to "[c]ast then from you our ornaments and put on your own armor; be men in shape, men in show, men in words, men in actions, men in counsel, men in example" (288). *Haec Vir*'s primary concern is to re-establish a societal order in which men act like men and women act like women, without having to take up masculine dress and attitudes in order to "preserve those manly things which [men] have forsaken" (288). The desire to return both men and women to their correct roles stems from a real sense of insecurity fostered by changing fashions for women in Jacobean England and by the perception of the effeminacy of the Jacobean court culture.

38. Painter, "Amazones," p. 161.

"Are You My Sweet Heart?": *Bonduca* and the Failure of Chivalric Masculinity
Andrew Bretz

Bonduca (1613) is a play about the effects of rape. The rapes of Bonduca's daughters are not merely presented as acts of horrendous violation; Fletcher presents the rapes as a form of bodily violation that is a necessary effect of the construction of chivalric masculinity. In such a vision of masculinity, the knight was always recoverable into patriarchal order, despite even the most horrific failures of masculine deportment. Rape is always both an act that sexually violates the individual and a part of a social script of patriarchal power and domination. One form that social script took in early modern England is the chivalric romance, where rape was integral to the creation and maintenance of a knightly identity. The good knight proved his masculinity by protecting damsels in distress from the ever-present threat of rape, whereas the fallen knight could redeem himself from an act of rape by reintegrating himself within the social script of normative heterosexuality through marriage. Kathryn Gravdal, for instance, argues that rape is an essential characteristic of the genre of chivalric romance.[1] Moreover, Corinne Saunders notes that not only was one of the primary chivalric romantic texts, *Le Morte D'Arthur*, written by a man convicted of rape, but it begins with a tale of rape.[2] Michael Hattaway argues that masculinity was at a crisis point in the early modern period and that chivalry – both a residual and a dominant ideology that articulated masculinity as a series of active achievements and femininity as a state of perpetual passiveness – was to account for such a crisis. That is, the movement from chivalric warrior to chivalric servant of a beloved, an essential structure of early modern understandings of chivalry, rendered the masculine subject effeminate.[3] The model of masculinity promulgated by chivalric romance has, at its heart, a narrative of sexual assault wherein the knight who rapes can be reintegrated into the prevailing patriarchal order, a narrative that Fletcher interrogates in *Bonduca* by refusing to provide the moment of reintegration.

This refusal to reintegrate the rapist into patriarchal order is perhaps unsurprising coming from Fletcher whose work, both with Beaumont and on his own, often lampooned and interrogated chivalric codes and ideals. The critical reception of *Bon-*

duca in the late twentieth century has been largely split: some see the play as the work of Coleridge's "servile jure divino Royalist,"[4] while others, following Finkelpearl's reading of *Philaster, A King and No King*, and *The Maid's Tragedy*,[5] recognize in the Fletcher canon an invitation to an ironic interpretation of plots and characters which seem to support a chivalric and Royalist agenda.[6] Even those critics who maintain the play is primarily reinforcing patriarchal chivalric ideologies, such as Jodi Mikalachki,[7] Simon Shepherd,[8] Paul D. Green,[9] and Sharon Macdonald,[10] recognize the play's ambivalence regarding the location of the audience's sympathies. Green, for instance, though arguing that Fletcher asks the audience to identify with Rome, admits that this "seems rather strange" given that the historical Boudicca "was traditionally lauded in England as a national heroine."[11] Whereas Bonduca's character, the leader of the British rebellion against the Roman imperium, defies easy categorization, even the brash militarism of Bonduca's cousin and general, Caratach, has been subject to ironic analysis. As Ronald Boling argues, Fletcher's critique of Caratach as the ideal chivalric soldier rests largely on his demythologized, monomaniacal adherence to a code of martial glory that comes at the expense of his community and his nation.[12] By the end of the play, following the disastrous rout of the British forces by the Romans, Caratach (whose character is so far removed from his historical namesake as to be unrecognizable) is beaten, starved, and finally imprisoned. In the end, he submits to the Roman governor, Swetonius, yet even that courtly submission is robbed of its impact by the very real lack that lingers over the stage. With the title character dead at the end of the fourth act, the rest of the play exists, as it were, in the shadow of her suicide. As in *Julius Caesar*, where Caesar's death removes the character from the play yet his presence lives on in the force he has over the actions of the other characters, Bonduca exists as a kind of imaginative presence in the final act. Bonduca's suicide with her daughters takes away the possibility for the redemption of Junius, the Roman knight and assaulter of Bonduca's second daughter. Their deaths, which encapsulate the incapacity for masculine governance in Britain, are a shame from which the men in the play cannot escape. Bonduca and her daughters emasculate the men of the play through their suicides so effectively that the fifth act serves as a final indictment of the performance of the chivalric masculine ideal. The central narratives of Junius' identity fail him and what is left is an uncompromisingly grim vision of chivalry, predicated upon sexual assault.

Chivalric Ideals

Chivalry sanitizes the violence of rape; it effaces the relationship between sexual violence and military aggression. For the chivalric knight, the man who rapes is an affront to patriarchal order and chivalric honour and is therefore either to be reincorporated into that same order through marrying his victim or being killed. The chivalric myth is one predicated on the construction of masculinity as a category of individual achievement, yet rape troubles the boundaries between individual and community. Rape is an act never wholly committed just against an individual; rather, rape affects the bonds that identify a community, which is why rape has historically been used as a weapon of war. Chivalric rape narratives reinforce the power of the father, the king, and the household by re-establishing the disrupted family ties and providing a means for both rapist and victim to exhibit exemplary patriarchal self-governance through the marriage of the rapist and the victim. In the supposedly benevolent paternalism of the chivalric code, the threat of rape is enough to justify the protection of women "for their own good" within the patriarchal household. The occasional appearance of women outside of the household within chivalric narratives (as knights, for instance) has the paradoxical effect of reinforcing this conservative image of community bonds. As Bourke states, "In a war where women could be combatants, manliness demand[s] particularly vigilant policing."[13] In *Bonduca*, however, the chivalric code that governs masculine behaviour towards women in terms of both protection and service has already failed and it is not protection that Bonduca and her daughters seek; they seek resistance against a patriarchal order predicated on sexual assault.

In the chivalric model of masculinity, rape is the most despicable act, yet is also the "natural" expression of aggressive masculine desire. This paradoxical attitude towards rape within the romantic tradition constructs a model of conflicted masculinity. Jocelyn Catty explains:

> Chivalric romance aestheticises rape as a normative male action. Although the standard pattern of rape and rescue normalizes rape predominantly as the practice of evil characters, several tendencies emerge which justify it in behavioural terms, rather than as a generic requirement. The troping of rape as an expression of love or uncontrollable desire … implicitly excuses rape even while condemning it.[14]

The masculine subject in the chivalric model is always expressing a conflicting set of desires. On the one hand, the knight requires the sexual assaulter as a worthy antagonist, yet the knight's own sexual desires within the script of chivalric chastity can only be expressed through rape. Indeed, as Catty shows, many of the chivalric romances of the late sixteenth century present repeated instances of the knight who commits rape being recovered into the normative model of heterosexuality through marriage.[15] The knight who raped, far from being a wholly abjected vision of masculinity in chivalric romance, was often a paradox of virtue and vice. For example, in *A Modern Lucretia*, Bandello constructed the knight who rapes as a man whose single vice (overweening sexual desire) "darkeneth the credit of a number of virtues!"[16] Just as it does for female characters, the rape becomes a test of the male character's virtuous nature. If the character attempted to recover himself into the heterosexual framework of marriage (by doing his victim the honour of marrying her), then his initial sexual assault could be justified within the context of the narrative. His predatory sexual desire would be domesticated within the marriage bonds. However, if the man who raped was unrepentant or (more often) his predatory acts of sexual desire were only potential rather than completed, then he could serve as a contrast for the virtuous knight.

The paradox of the chivalric narrative of the knight who rapes, yet who returns to the normative fold through marrying his victim, can be clarified by understanding how chivalric romance understood the worth of a knight. The virtue of the knight is not exclusively proven by his martial valour – though that certainly is a part of the construction of chivalric subject – rather, as Kenneth Hodges points out, the knight's worth is expressed through his adherence to a cause: "[The knight] proves his commitment to other causes – honor, justice, a claim to a given piece of land, an assertion that one woman is the most beautiful – not by injury to the loser but by injury on his side: to his own body or to those who matter to him."[17] A knight's valour does not come from his ability to remain impervious to wounds, but to bear them, and bear the thought that they are yet to come. Hodges continues, "even if the winner is not in fact hurt, his knowledge that he might be is critical. Real risk, understood in advance, can show a combatant's commitment to a cause."[18] It is the ability of the knight to endure, to remain faithful to a cause that marks his valour in chivalric romance. The wounds he sustains are external evidence of his endurance and faith. If he were emotionally wounded by an act of sexual forcing, then that would provide after-the-fact evidence for his faith to the woman he raped, and therefore his emotional wounds could be transformed into chivalric valour by reinserting himself into the normative script of romance and marriage. The emotional wounds may be self-inflicted by lack of personal governance, but their presence implies a kind of emotional "faith," within the logic of chivalric romance.

Chivalric romances of the medieval and early modern period repeatedly deploy the sexual assaulter-as-villain trope as it gave structure to both male virility and female virtue. The more villainous the man who raped, the more heroic the knight is who defeats him, but, also the more chaste the victim who successfully deflects that man's advances. Such a narrative structure is inherently contradictory. That is, the arch-narrative of assault in chivalric romance positioned the victim of rape as not virtuous enough to defend herself against her assaulter. As Jocelyn Catty notes, this paradoxical vision of romantic femininity is based on the premise that it was nearly impossible to rape women forcibly. This myth emerged from understandings of anatomy and biology available at the time, which can be summed up in the nineteenth-century concept "it is impossible to sheathe a sword in a vibrating scabbard."[19] This vision of rape, which Catty calls yielding rape, meant that heterosexual coitus could not happen unless the female partner on some level consented to the sexual act. The victim in this chivalric narrative of rape does not resist unto death, but takes pity on the strenuous exertions of the man committing the assault and eventually allows him to sexually abuse her. Though still rape, despite the act of enforced or coerced consent, yielding rape at least provided a mechanism to understand why rape could happen in the first place, given that women's bodies were posited as un-rapable by many early modern texts. G. Rivers in 1639 used precisely this argument when describing the rape of Lucrece: "This revenge may argue chastitie before and after: but not in the nick of the act, which yeelding to some secret enticement might staine her thought; then loathing her selfe for the act, held death a more satisfactory revenge then repentence."[20] Yielding rape figured a woman's body as an impregnable fortress, only accessible when she deigned to give the male assaulter access. The victim's "mercy" for her assaulter contrasted with her adherence to chastity, which was the normative virtue of femininity in the early modern period.

In this romantic/chivalric narrative of sexual assault, the man who committed rape was never wholly culpable for the rape, as the rape was always in some sense a mutual sexual act. Caratach, in 3.5, suggests precisely this explanation for the rapes of Bonduca's daughters when, after he foils their attempts at seeking revenge against the men who raped them, he directly blames them:

> 2 Daughter   By —— Uncle,
> We will have vengeance for our rapes.
>
> Caratach   By ——
> You should have kept your legs closed then; dispatch there.[21]

The paradoxical logic of victim-blaming and the contradictory construction of the feminine erotic identity – chaste, but yielding – was mirrored in the contradictory construction of masculine erotic identity – predatory, yet protective. Caratach's expression of solidarity towards the Roman enemy undermines this romantic structure of protection/predation as he seems wholly uninterested in defending the honour of Bonduca's daughters and only wishes to test his manliness on the field of battle. It is the character of Junius, however, who exemplifies the paradox of the predatory/protective structure of chivalric masculine identity.

In *Bonduca*, the rapes of Bonduca's daughters happen prior to the narrative, so the rapist against whom the virtuous knight (Junius) can test his mettle appears to be unknown. I suggest, however, that Junius is functionally both the knight errant and the knight who raped Bonduca's second daughter, Bonvica. Junius spends the first two acts playing the grief-stricken lover, attempting to reinsert himself into the normative script of romance and marriage. For this, he is roundly mocked by Petillius while Swetonius declares, "sure his own discretion will reclaim him, / He must deserve our anger else" (1.2.272-3). Junius, the chivalric lover, presents a form of wounded subjectivity that must be recovered into healthy masculine expression. This can either be through, as Swetonius suggests, increased self-discipline and integration into an all-male system of martial aggression, or through reintegration into a system of normative heterosexuality suggested by the chivalric mode. Though his love for his maiden fair, Bonduca's second daughter, is experienced by him as a form of attack, the nature of which precludes response, his "faith" to her expresses the possibility of Junius' chivalric valour.[22]

That Junius is more than merely a grief-stricken lover and, indeed, is the man who raped Bonduca's second daughter, is suggested in the course of the piece, though never explicitly stated. In act three, the daughters of Bonduca send Junius a letter, claiming that Bonvica returns the love that he bears to her. When Junius arrives with a small company of Romans, Bonvica and her sister take the Romans captive and mock them mercilessly for having believed that Bonvica could ever love Junius. Though this scene (3.5) can be read as merely tormenting or teasing the Romans, the second daughter's words suggest a kind of metatheatrical awareness of the generic constraints of the chivalric romance:

> Are you my sweet heart?
> It looks ill on't: how long is't pretty soul,
> Since you and I first lov'd? Had we not reason
> To doat extreamly upon one another?(3.5.31-4)

She comments on the scene, noting how the context has shifted from the romantic to the martial immediately before she appeals to the initial moment of desire, described as "love." Earlier in the play, Junius claimed "shee has been ravish'd" (2.2.34), describing the rape in the passive voice, which rhetorically weakens his own moral responsibility. Nevertheless, it seems that here Bonduca's second daughter is mocking a man who is infatuated with her, and she is also pointing specifically to an originary moment of violation that parallels the emasculation of the soldiers that she is undertaking in the scene. She speaks to Junius in the discourse of chivalric love – that he is her "pretty soul" and that they "first lov'd" and thus they should "doat extreamly" upon one another – only to mock Junius's desire for her. Indeed, appearing at the heart of act three, this scene forms the structural climax to the play. Further, it is the scene in which the nature of the fundamental crime of the play is contested. To the daughters of Bonduca, the play's motivating crime is the rape that happened before the play began, aligning the narrative with the generic markers of Jacobean revenge tragedy. As Julie Crawford states, however,

> The crime in this play, according to Caratach, is disarming men, not rape. What was historically the virtuous heroism of Boadicea's daughters (avenging their rapes, which were also conceived of as a violation of their nation), is replaced by Caratach's assertion of their inherent culpability and weakness: they should have kept their legs closed. Through this judgment, Caratach also makes it clear that his alliance is with soldiers – even enemy soldiers – not women, and that he is concerned less with female honor, or national vengeance, than he is with male honor.[23]

Bonduca's second daughter is avenging her own rape in this scene by emasculating the Romans. She focuses not upon any Romans, or even a Roman who is infatuated with her, but with the man who raped her, a rape which she sarcastically describes as when "you and I first lov'd." Though no one in the play claims unequivocally that Junius raped Bonduca's second daughter, what she says in this scene makes available a reading in which Junius is the man who raped her.

As Junius presents himself within the narrative tradition of the chivalric lover, he does not require a male enemy of equal valour to pit himself against in combat to prove himself. His "proof" comes from his ability to express his faith for Bonvica. The exemplary failure of Junius – being trapped by the plot of the daughters of Bonduca in act three – visualizes Junius' courtly subjection to Bonvica and highlights the irony of chivalric gender relations. The lover's rhetoric of self-abnegation becomes starkly real as Bonvica threatens to torture and kill him. For Junius, the rape of Bonduca's daughters helps him construct himself as a chivalric subject through the expression of romantic "love" and "faith," yet the play reveals this subject position to be ultimately an untenable failure that cannot be maintained in the face of the trauma caused by rape itself.

Sacrifice and Suicide

The dehumanization inherent in rape is echoed in historians' accounts of the rebellion of Boudicca. Though the daughters' names are never given by historians, Fletcher does offer a name for at least the second daughter.[24] In her self-penned letter to Junius, she signs herself "Bonvica." Indeed, since the name is read aloud, it becomes more resonant and her character more individuated with a theatrical audience than would be possible if it were merely a speech heading. One can read the second daughter of Bonduca, the object of Junius's affections, as a subject of the yielding rape described by Catty or as an attempt to subvert the normative expectations of early modern femininity, through her initial rejection of the demand to commit suicide. Given that suicide was the normative model for feminine comportment after a rape (viz. Lucretia), and given that Bonduca and her daughters commit suicide, it would seem that after three acts of resistance to normative patriarchal roles and narratives, what is going on in the fourth act is a re-alignment of Bonduca and her daughters in terms of feminine chastity. This reading, however, fails to note the reactions of the Romans to the suicides and the explicit reasons for the suicides themselves.

Act four presents an allegorized version of the rapes that started the revolt. Bonduca and her daughters, along with the remaining British forces, seek refuge within a castle, while the Roman forces lay siege. The situation – an assailed castle with masculine besiegers begging for mercy from the feminine occupants of the castle – embodies the structure of yielding rape within the chivalric mode of masculinity. For Bonduca and her daughters to choose death rather than rape would be to deny the assailants a form of masculine redemption only available through completing the narrative. The catapults and phallic battering rams assault the walls while the Roman general Swetonius parlays for surrender using the discourse of chivalric romance and love:

> DECIUS   Yeeld, Queen.
> BONDUCA I am unacquainted with that language, Roman.
> SWETONIUS Yeeld, honour'd Lady, and expect our mercie.
>   We love thy noblenesse.
> BONDUCA   I thank ye, ye say well;
>   But mercie and love are sins in Rome and hell.
> SWETONIUS Ye cannot scape our strength; ye must yeeld, Ladie,
>   Ye must adore and fear the power of Rome.(4.4.8-14)

Bonduca rejects the language of yielding, of a chivalry predicated on the vision of the yielding rape. The female body in chivalric romance is figured as a fortress and Swetonius' caution to Bonduca that he will take mercy on her if she yields perversely replays the rape of Bonduca's daughters. Bonduca, however, plays on Swetonius' use of the term "mercy" to expose the moral poverty of the chivalric romantic discourse, which leads into Swetonius's appeal not to love or affection but to power and fear. Throughout this section, the term "mercy" is repeated with subtle differences in meaning in the mouths of Bonduca, her second daughter, and Swetonius. Indeed, the various ways that "mercy" is used suggest that what is at stake here is the authority of the multiple meanings of the term "mercy." In refusing Swetonius' "mercy," Bonduca refuses to participate in the script of yielding rape, revealing the terms of such a script to be predicated upon violence and horror. Swetonius' sudden shift in rhetorical mood exposes the rapes as explicit strategies of patriarchal domination. Bonduca revels in this admission,

> If Rome be earthly, why should any knee
> With bending adoration worship her?
> She's vitious; and your partiall selves confesse,
> Aspires the height of all impietie:
> Therefore 'tis fitter I should reverence
> The thatched houses where the Britains dwell
> In carelesse mirth, where the blest household gods
> See nought but chaste and simple puritie.(4.4.15-22)

Robbed of the fiction of feminine complicity in sexual assault, Swetonius' appeal to violence exposes Rome and, by extension, the chivalric masculine identity as morally impoverished. Bonduca's final lines offer a contrary vision of civilization that points to the suicide of Bonduca's daughters: "sacred thoughts in holy bosoms stor'd / Make people noble, and the place ador'd"(4.4.25-6).

When the siege continues, Bonduca and her daughters commit suicide rather than fall into Roman captivity; however, Bonvica is more reluctant than her sister or mother. She asks her mother to "speak gently / To these fierce men, they will afford ye pitie"(4.4.29-30), and in doing so raises the problem of her own complicity in her rape . By asking her mother to conform more explicitly to a normative model of femininity, she implies that she herself did so during her own rape. If her rape was a form of yielding, then the logical romance narrative's conclusion would be for Junius and her to wed, reinforcing the structures of chivalric masculinity that Junius has ascribed to the whole play. This narrative seems to be at play as Bonduca's second daughter appeals to the Romans to save her, which causes Bonduca to label her "whore"(4.4.99); yet Fletcher manipulates the narrative structure to deny such a conclusion . Bonvica's consent would not simply invalidate the rebellion, but at the same time would validate the vision of Junius' chivalric masculinity. The actual reasons for Bondvica's initial refusal to commit suicide have less to do with the validation of chivalric masculinity and more to do with the trauma caused by rape.

> 1 DAUGHTER   Do it, worthy sister:
>   'Tis nothing, 'tis a pleasure; we'll go with ye.
> 2 DAUGHTER O if I knew but whither.

> 1 DAUGHTER   To the blessed,
>   Where we shall meet our father.
> SWETONIUS   Woman.
> BONDUCA   Talk not.
> 1 DAUGHTER Where nothing but true joy is.
> BONDUCA   That's a good wench,
>   Mine own sweet girl; put it close to thee.
> 2 DAUGHTER O comfort me still, for heavens sake.
> 1 DAUGHTER   Where eternal
>   Our youths are, and our beauties; where no Wars come,
>   *Nor lustful slaves to ravish us.*
> 2 DAUGHTER   That steels me:
>   A long farewell to this world.(4.4.104-113, emphasis mine)

One sister tries to comfort the other sister to the inevitability of suicide. Instead of inscribing the daughters of Bonduca within a patriarchal system of governance, however, the suicide allows them to escape that system. The suicides are an act of self-agency, defying the attempted masculine policing of the feminine body by Swetonius and the Romans. In this dialogue, the patriarch (Swetonius) attempts to interrupt the women's speech but is immediately shouted down by Bonduca herself. The first daughter describes a heaven without war and the rape that is used as a weapon of war, where they will be reunited with their dead father, Prasutagus. Bonvica fears death, but can be brought to kill herself when she is assured that the men who raped her cannot follow them into a heavenly afterlife. The trauma and violence of rape is reinforced through this final act of resistance. It is the fear of a violation that might continue after death that keeps her alive, and it is her sister's comforting reassurance that in heaven they cannot be sexually assaulted that "steels" her to death.

Bonvica's action is contextualized against the ideals of normative femininity from Roman antiquity, thus reinforcing that this suicide ought to be contrasted against traditional, normative visions. The first daughter references Portia and Lucrece, both of whom she finds lacking, but Lucrece's suicide in particular she associates not with the resolution of epistemic ambiguity regarding her rape, but a suicidal despair brought on by desire.

>   Your great Saint Lucrece
> Di'd not for honour; Tarquin topt her well,
> And mad she could not hold him, bled.(4.4.117-19)

Though, as Ian Donaldson notes, this vision of Lucrece as a lustful woman was certainly not unique (36-7); it is an extravagant mockery of Lucrece by one who wishes to belittle a Roman heroine in favour of a more honourable Briton. Further, the description sits in contrast to the suicide the audience has just witnessed. Bonduca's second daughter resolutely refuses to allow the natural conclusion of the narrative of chivalric romance – marriage to the man who raped her. Even though Junius has already made it clear that he has no interest in her any longer, the generic requirements of chivalric romance demand that the two should be together by the end of the play; her suicide is a radical disengagement with the genre. Though the story of Lucrece is a clear inspiration for the dramatic presentation of Bonvica's suicide, Bonduca's first daughter re-configures Lucrece as a character from untouchable and glorified saint to a leaky vessel of desire. Not only are the cultural differences separating Romans and Britons underscored, but Bonduca's first daughter posits a uniquely British femininity predicated on unyielding resistance to rape and dishonour, even unto death. This model of femininity subverts the chivalric model of masculinity, built upon a narrative of yielding rape and ultimate reintegration into the dominant patriarchal order through marrying the rape victim.

If the death of Bonduca's second daughter shakes the Roman forces gathered below the castle, Bonduca's own suicide shatters them, for it solidifies the presentation of a feminine identity characterized by uncompromising resistance to the chivalric narratives that feed colonial expansion. Intending to poison herself, Bonduca addresses first her daughters, then the Romans,

> BONDUCA I come, wench; to ye all Fates hang-men; you
>   That ease the aged destinies, and cut
>   The threds of Kingdoms, as they draw 'em: here,
>   Here's a draught would ask no less then Caesar
>   To pledge it for the glories sake.
>
> CURIUS   Great Lady.
>
> SWETONIUS Make up your own conditions.
>
> BONDUCA   So we will.
>
> SWETONIUS Stay.
>
> DEMETRIUS   Stay.
>
> SWETONIUS   Be any thing.(4.4.134-9)

If Bonduca dies, the Romans would be robbed of a triumph over an enemy, but more importantly, if Bonduca kills herself then she will have created a feminine subject position that discredits the chivalric narrative of the re-integration of the sexually deviant knight who rapes into the dominant patriarchal order that the Romans have been pursuing all along. They beg her to live, offering her the chance to "be any thing," yet one must assume that "any thing" would be circumscribed within the scope of patriarchal order. Either that, or the Romans are begging her to live as part of a strategy to allow them to be the ones who kill her rather than allowing her to take her own life. When she does kill herself, she does so employing the medical discourse of birth, turning the gender relations of semen/spirit/soul and womb/body/flesh on their head:

> I hate to prosecute my victory,
> That I will give ye counsel ere I die.
> If you will keep your Lawes and Empire whole,

> Place in your Romane flesh a Britain soul.(4.4.150-4)

By subverting the narrative of chivalric romance, Bonduca and her daughters leave Junius and the other Romans with no ideological support for their colonization of Britain, save the paradoxical and gender-bending instruction to "place in your Romane flesh a Britain soul." Further, this admonition leaves the Romans with no clear vision of a legitimate form of masculine self-governance, as the chivalric form has been discredited. The rest of the play exists as it were in the shadow of the trio of suicides that end act four, scene four. Masculinity remains the theme, yet there is no conclusion as to what form the masculine must take in a world where the feminine is characterized by resistance. The attempts by Junius and Petillius to recover their tarnished masculine honour and Caratach's eventual capture cannot recover the narrative thread that was lost with the death of Bonduca and her daughters. The fifth act presents the attempt to reassert masculine dominance, but this attempt takes place in a world notably devoid of women, where the hyper-masculine Caratach is forced to become nursemaid to the child Hengo. When the Romans finally capture Caratach, Swetonius gives orders that "Through the Camp in every tongue, / The Vertues of great Caratach be sung" (5.3.201-2), yet there is something more than a little odd about the total exclusion of the eponymous character from the final laudatory songs.[25] Though there is an attempt to re-establish homosocial order, without a feminine (or in Hengo's case, troped feminine) object of exchange, the praises of the men are hollow echoes of patriarchal governance.

Bonduca does not provide a space for a renovated, virtuous patriarchal state. Rome is frustrated in its attempts to capture Bonduca for a triumph, and the elimination of all women in the play forces Caratach into the position of mother and nurse to the juvenile Hengo. Rome is neither renovated nor recuperated into a virtuous patriarchal order, nor is the only surviving Briton, Caratach. Though the Romans do indeed succeed in putting down the rebellion, the suicides of Bonduca and her daughters frustrate their success. They refuse to situate themselves within a new Roman order. Fletcher ends the play with Roman forces leading off Caratach to captivity, appealing to an offstage triumph, yet to occur. This is ultimately ironic, however, as such a triumph would celebrate a failure to recuperate a man who raped, and a failure to renovate the system that enabled the man to rape.

Impossible Recovery

Bonduca first took the stage in 1613, performed by the King's Men in the aftermath of the death of Prince Henry, when the young man who had embodied the Jacobean chivalric ideal had been struck down, thus opening up the possibility of ironic critique of such an ideal. The play presents the rape of Bonvica as the exemplary failure of one of the most valorized narratives of masculine governance in the early modern period – the knightly lover. Junius cannot complete the master-narrative of recovery into the patriarchal order that is dictated by the chivalric model of masculinity and marry the woman he raped. Her resistance subverts the fiction of compliance at the heart of yielding rape. He attempts to reassert his masculinity through martial valour, yet even this rings hollow after the bravura performance of Bonduca. The rape lingers over the fifth act as an unresolvable crime in the chivalric mode. It is here that, for the first time, there is something beginning to approach a modern concept of the assaulter as rapist rather than merely as a man who raped, for it is here – when the knight is unable to restore patriarchal order despite the total exclusion of women – that the act of raping another human being becomes an identity from which Junius cannot escape.

Notes

1. Kathryn Gravdal, *Ravishing Maidens: Writing Rape in Medieval French Literature and Law.* (Philadelphia: University of Pennsylvania Press, 1991) pp. 43-4.
2. Corinne Saunders, *Rape and Ravishment in the Literature of Medieval England.* (London, New York: Routledge, 1998), pp. 234-41.
3. Michael Hattaway, "Male Sexuality and Misogyny," in *Shakespeare and Sexuality*, ed. Catherine M.S. Alexander and Stanley Wells. (Cambridge: Cambridge University Press, 2001), pp. 92-115, at 108-09.
4. Samuel Taylor Coleridge, *Coleridge on the Seventeenth Century.* ed. Roberta Florence Brinkley. (Durham: Duke University Press, 1955), p. 655.
5. Philip Finkelpearl, *Court and Country Politics in the Work of Beaumont and Fletcher.* (Princeton: Princeton University Press, 1990), pp. 146ff.
6. Suzanne Gossett, "Introduction," to Francis Beaumont and John Fletcher, *Philaster* (London: Methuen, 2009), p. 25.
7. Jodi Mikalachki, *The Legacy of Boadicea: Gender and Nation in Early Modern England.* (London: Routledge, 1998), pp. 96ff.
8. Simon Shepherd, *Amazons and Warrior Women: Varieties of Feminism in Seventeenth-Century Drama* (New York: St. Martin's Press, 1981), p. 149.
9. Paul D. Green, "Theme and Structure in Fletcher's *Bonduca*," *Studies in English Literature, 1500-1900* 22.2(1982): 305-316.
10. Sharon Macdonald, "Boadicea: Warrior, Mother, and Myth," in *Images of Women in War and Peace: Perspectives.* ed. Sharon Macdonald, Pat Holden, and Shirley Ardener. (Madison: University of Wisconsin Press, 1988), x-xx, at p. 281.
11. Green, "Theme and Structure," pp. 307-8.
12. Roland J. Boling, "Fletcher's Satire of Caratach in 'Bonduca,'" *Comparative Drama* 33.3(1999): 390-407.
13. Joanna Bourke, *Rape: A History from 1860 to the Present.* (London: Virago, 2007), p. 375.
14. Jocelyn Catty, *Writing Rape, Writing Women in Early Modern England.* (New York: Palgrave MacMillan, 2010), p. 28.
15. Catty, *Writing Rape*, p. 29.
16. Matteo Bandello, "A Modern Lucretia," in *Tragical Tales: The Complete Novels.* ed. Hugh Harris, and tr. Geoffrey Fenton. (London: Routledge, 1923), p. 340. The early modern stage abounds with instances of a character who commits rape being presented as a largely virtuous man, with the exception of the one act of sexual assault and/or attempted sexual assault. Cf. *Measure for Measure, Ram Alley, The Double Falsehood, The Rover.*
17. Kenneth Hodges, "Wound ed Masculinity: Injury and Gender in Sir Thomas Malory's *Le Morte D'Arthur*," *Studies in Philology* 106(2009): 13-31, at p. 13.
18. Hodges "Wounded Masculinity," p.13
19. Joanna Bourke, "Rape Myths Past and Present." *New Statesman.* 10 March 2008. http://www.newstatesman.com/life-and-society/2008/03/rape-myths-women-stump-sexual. Accessed 15 July 2015.

20. Quoted from Ian Donaldson, *The Rapes of Lucretia: A Myth and its Transformations*. (Oxford: Claredon Press, 1982), p. 37.

21. *Bonduca* (Bowers), 3.5.68-71.

22. It is possible that through the "love" plot of Junius and Bonduca's second daughter Fletcher is obliquely alluding to or commenting upon the tradition of lovers from warring factions, like that in Shakespeare's *Romeo and Juliet*. If that is the case, however, Fletcher's play offers a far more pessimistic vision of erotic desire and the ability to mend political fractures through appealing to the traditions of romantic, courtly love than is presented in Shakespeare.

23. Julie Crawford, "Fletcher's *The Tragedie of Bonduca* and the Anxieties of the Masculine Government of James I," *SEL Studies in English Literature 1500-1900* 39.2(1999): 357-81, at p. 363

24. Holinshed, *Chronicles*, quoted from *The Holinshed Project: The Texts*. ed. Richard Rowley. (London, 1587). http://www.english.ox.a.uk?holinshed/texts.php?texttext1=1587_0166. Accessed 15 July 2015. pp51-5. Tacitus, *The Annals of Tacitus*. Tr. Alfred J. Church and William J. Brodribb. (London: MacMillan & Co., 1879): 14.24-39. Cassius Dio, *Dio's Roman History* Tr. Earnest Cary. Vol. 8 (Cambridge, MA: Harvard University Press, 1961), 62.1-12. Fletcher clearly draws from Holinshed's 1577 edition of *The Chronicles* for many of the speeches and details of his narrative, yet Holinshed does not provide a name for either daughter. In this, he is following the practice of classical historians of the rebellion such as Cassius Dio and Tacitus, neither of whom provide names for the daughters.

25. The performance history of the play shows multiple examples of the fourth and fifth acts being conflated or reworked such that Bonduca and her daughters die immediately before Caratach's capture. Thus, her occlusion in performances such as Purcell's semi-opera and Colman's 1778 adaptation is not quite as jarring as it is in the original text.

Mucedorus, Shakespeare, and the Persistence of Romance

Dimitry Senyshyn

*M*ost scholarly discussions of *Mucedorus* begin by pointing out how little scholarly attention the play has received; for anyone working in the academic Shakespeare industry, this is an unusual and pleasant condition in which to find a play. We are advised that *Mucedorus* has been largely relegated to footnotes, its chief interest lying in its universally assumed popularity and its alleged relationship to Shakespeare. Over the centuries, various critics have ascribed the play as a whole, though more often in part, to Shakespeare, listing it among the "Shakespeare Apocrypha." Recently, Eric Rasmussen and Jonathan Bate released an edition of Shakespeare apocrypha, including *Mucedorus*, in which they claim, with the aid of computer software, to have detected Shakespeare's "fingerprints" in several instances.[1] There is, of course, no external evidence linking Shakespeare to the play, other than the fact that the title page of the 1610 quarto attributes authorship to "William Sh.," and that he was working with the King's Men when they presented it at court, presumably with additions, on a Shrove Sunday night before the printing of the 1610 edition. In general, scholars eager to expand the Shakespeare canon find the bard's fingerprints on *Mucedorus* to a degree commensurate either with their esteem for the play or their zeal to support a particular narrative about the development of Shakespeare's career or of the King's Men's repertory. While the King of Valentia is given some fine lines in the 1610 additions, I do not intend to ascribe them to Shakespeare, though it would only positively impact my argument were he to turn out to have written them. What I would like to do is to offer my own narrative, taking into account the play's popularity, its framing narrative, and the additions of 1610 in order to offer some tentative thoughts about *Mucedorus*' significance to the development of Shakespeare's tragicomedies and his generic turn toward romance around 1608.

Edward Dowden's romanticized characterization of Shakespeare's late plays – *Pericles*, *Cymbeline*, *The Winter's Tale*, and *The Tempest* – as being the mellow fruits of a mature, backwards-looking imagination that eschewed the cynicism of the great tragedies for more redemptive narratives is unsatisfying.[2] Scholars such as Reginald Foakes and Arthur Kirsch have attempted to account for the development of Shakespeare's romantic tragicomedies as a response to the vogue for court masques and the experimental tragicomedies of the so-called "coterie theatres" occupied by companies like the Children of the Queen's Revels. When John Fletcher's pastoral tragicomedy *The Faithful Shepherdess* was premiered by the Children of the Revels in 1608, it was a terrible flop. In the manner of many responsible Jacobean playwrights, he responded with righteous outrage in a note "to the reader" in a published text of the play, explaining how his audience's ignorance of tragicomic form led them to misunderstand and therefore dismiss his work. In his preface, Fletcher essentially paraphrased the principles of tragicomedy outlined by Giambattista Guarini in his *Compendium of Tragicomic Poetry* (1601), which was itself written in defense of Guarini's *Il Pastor Fido* (1590), Fletcher's primary source for his play:

> ...It is a pastorall Tragi-comedie, which the people seeing when it was plaid, having ever had a singular guift in defining, concluded to be a play of country hired Shepheards in gray cloakes, with curtaild dogs in strings, sometimes laughing together, and sometimes killing one another...A tragic-comedie is not so called in respect of mirth and killing, but in respect it wants deaths, which is inough to make it no tragedie, yet brings some neere it, which is inough to make it no comedie: which must be a representation of familiar people, with such kinde of trouble as no life be questioned, so that a God is as lawfull in this as in a tragedie, and meane people as in a comedie.³

In respect of mirth and killing, *Mucedorus* has plenty of both; its characters run the gamut of class, between familiar persons and the mighty, and though the troubles of its heroes are framed to the extent that none of their lives is seriously questioned, the threat of death is met at several turns, and several bodies do fall on stage; the comically flippant manner in which they are dispatched, however, guarantees that the play is no tragedy. While *Mucedorus* clearly fails to meet Fletcher's early criteria for the ideal tragicomedy, it seems as if a play like *Mucedorus* is just what Fletcher imagines his audience to have been anticipating – a pastoral gallimaufry, or what Philip Sidney would call a "mungrell Tragy-comedie".⁴

Lucy Munro suggests that Fletcher's defence here is not of tragicomedy as a whole, but of his specific play in the face of its theatrical failure.⁵ She goes on to argue that a handful of plays in the Children of the Queen's Revels' repertory helped to create the foundations of the Fletcherian form of tragicomedy that would dominate the later Jacobean and Caroline stage. Plays like *The Malcontent* and *The Isle of Gulls* that combined comedy and tragedy, pastoral and satirical railing would, along with their implicit acknowledgment of Guarini's principles of tragicomedy, help to develop what amounted to a house style of tragicomedy in the Children of the Queen's Revels' repertory. While this is a fine theory and is helpful in contextualizing the dramaturgy of Fletcher's *Faithful Shepherdess*, I would propose extending her idea that certain works "form a pervasive background…in which source texts are assimilated into a complex cultural network" beyond the repertory of the Children of the Revels.[6] After all, in 1607-8, the year of *Faithful Shepherdess'* theatrical failure, a very different kind of tragicomedy was being offered at the Globe.

Pericles, which would prove to be Shakespeare's most popular play in print – appearing in eight separate editions by 1685 – borrows from the conventions of Greek and English romance along with saints' plays and other genres, and its tone runs the gamut from the farcical to the tragic to the sublime. It is self-consciously old-fashioned in its verse form and its incorporation of a narrative chorus, and it contains the sort of fantastical elements associated with the dramatic romances that crowded the London stage in the 1570s and '80s. Harbage's *Annals* for this period includes thirty-one titles that suggest a generic affinity with the romance tradition. Sadly, only three of these plays have survived: *Sir Clyomon and Sir Clamydes* (c.1570), *Common Conditions* (c.1576) and The *Rare Triumphs of Love and Fortune* (1582). But, judging from the scornful criticism heaped upon dramatic romance by George Whetstone, Stephen Gosson, Philip Sidney and John Lyly, these plays appear to be representative of their genre.[7] In the *Defence of Poesy* (1583), Sidney's complaint about the impoverished state of English drama is lodged in terms that directly address what he perceives as the dramaturgically unsophisticated conventions of the popular romance genre. While he finds a certain disregard for narrative plausibility and aesthetic coherence in *Gorboduc*, a play he admires, he asks:

> ...if it be so in *Gorboduc*, how much more in all the rest? where you shall have Asia of the one side, and Afric of the other, and so many other under-kingdoms, that the player, when he cometh in, must ever begin with telling where he is, or else the tale will not be conceived. Now ye shall have three ladies walk to gather flowers, and then we must believe the stage to be a garden. By and by we hear news of shipwreck in the same place, and then we are to blame if we accept it not for a rock. Upon the back of that comes out a hideous monster with fire and smoke, and then the miserable beholders are bound to take it for a cave. While in the mean time two armies fly in, represented with four swords and bucklers, and then what hard heart will not receive it for a pitched field?[8]

If none of *Pericles'* characters are ever pursued by a dragon or a bear, its picaresque action nonetheless spans large temporal and geographical expanses, and its absorptive generic framework allows for deaths, a resurrection effected by musical therapy, the stage direction "Enter pirates," and a profoundly moving scene of familial reconciliation and redemption. Its blend of artifice, generic hybridity, and theatrical self-consciousness might be seen in some respects to align it with the tragicomedies of the Children's company, but its disregard for the Guarinian tragicomic formula, its lack of satirical edge, its often elegiac tone, its self-conscious archaism, and its reliance on the conventions, narratives, and thematic preoccupations of romance rather than those of Italianate pastoral mark it as being more closely aligned with the English tradition of early romance drama, exemplified by plays like *Mucedorus*, *The Rare Triumphs of Love and Fortune*, and *Sir Clyomon and Sir Clamydes*.

Dimitry Senyshyn

The epilogue of *Mucedorus*' 1610 quarto provides a tantalizing narrative that suggests that when Shakespeare's company performed the play at court, the King's Men were actively trying to distance themselves from the subject matter and dramatic style of the boys' companies. After the lovers are joined in marriage, the families reunited, and Segasto reformed at the play's conclusion, Envy acts. Apparently bested by his comic nemesis, he threatens to raise up "a Wretch, / A leane and hungry Neager Canniball…a Poet," with a "needie Beard"–often identified as Ben Jonson, who famously, supposedly, had trouble growing one – whom he will "whet on to write a Comedie, / Wherein shall be composd darke sentences, / Pleasing to factious braines":[9] just the sort of controversial railing satire for which the boys' companies were known and occasionally punished. Envy goes on to say he will play the tale-bearer, and report "Unto a puisant Magistrate" these "gaules, / (with some additions) so lately vented in your Theater". Comedy refutes him immediately, saying,

> This is a trap for Boyes, not Men, nor such,
> Especially desertfull in their doinges,
> Whose stay'd discretion rules their purposes.
> I and my faction do eschew those vices: (f.3v)

She then goes on to address King James, asking him to "Vouchsafe to pardon our unwilling error, / So late presented to your Gracious view, / And we'll endeavour with excess of pain, / To please your senses in a choicer strain" f.3v. It would seem that the King's Men had unintentionally offended their patron at some point and here have invoked the very spirit of discord and envy to excuse themselves, offering *Mucedorus* as a pleasing alternative to the offensive matter they recently presented. While the additions of 1610 literally dramatize the King's Men's attempt to dissociate themselves from the controversial qualities of coterie drama, their 1610 production of *Mucedorus* might be seen to perform their at least temporary abjuration of coterie playing styles and dramaturgies.

Richard T. Thornberry compellingly argues that changes in the epilogue and title page to the second quarto of *Mucedorus* suggest that there was a London performance sometime between 9 April 1604 and the publication of the revised play-text in 1606.[10] If there *was* a London performance before the King's Men's 1610 remount, then *Mucedorus*' durability as a performance piece may well have recommended old-fashioned romance as a fiscally viable genre for Shakespeare to experiment with, along with his likely co-author George Wilkins, when they began writing *Pericles*. If not, then the play, in print at least, held sufficient interest to warrant the publisher's decision to hazard a new edition in 1606. Box office prospects aside, however, the aspect of *Mucedorus* that I imagine to have most informed Shakespeare's developing experimentation with romance and tragicomedy is to be found in the interplay between the framing narrative and the main action. It is here that *Mucedorus*' ostensibly transparent dramaturgy combines with its deft manipulation of generically opposed signifiers in order to create tonally dissonant and powerful, localized theatrical effects. When Comedy first enters, dressed in the iconographical trappings of the genre she embodies, she makes clear her intent to make us laugh – a modest goal, consistent with her character and her affirmation that "Mirth is tollerable"[11], but the appearance of Envy, whose blood-smeared arms associate him with allegorical stage representations of Tragedy and whose diction associates him specifically with the Senecan tragedy of blood, seeks to "interrupt [her] tale, / And mixe [her] Musicke with a tragicke end"(A3r). Their elemental confrontation seems simple enough; theatrical opposites, both are single-mindedly and arbitrarily bent on exerting their influence over the generic identity of the play. However stark their differences in diction, tone, and intent, they both employ the language of conflict, and, intriguingly, both invoke gods of war. While Comedy calls upon Bellona's sweet breath and silver-tuned strings to aid her cause (A3r), Envy proclaims that Mars himself shall "breathe down / A peerless crown" upon his head and "raise his chivall with a lasting fame" (A3v). Mars and Bellona, often paired in iconographical representations, are here two sides of the same ideological coin, and Envy's use of the word "chivall" seems to anticipate the play's romantic mode. After a lengthy spell of sabre-rattling, Comedy asks Envy to forbear, to which he answers:

> Why so I will; forbeare shall be such
> As treble death shall crosse thee with despight,
> And make thee mourne where most thou joyest,
> Turning thy mirth into a deadly dole…
> This will I do, thus shall I bear with thee;
> And more to vex thee with a deeper spite,
> I will with threats of blood begin thy Play,
> Favouring thee with Envie and with Hate (A3v)

And Envy makes good on his word. "Treble death" is exactly what the play delivers, in the slaughter of Tremelio, Bremo, and the bear, and yet Envy's efforts do not upset the generic identity of the play; rather, they facilitate the comedy – a point which is driven home by the cast list's doubling of Envy with Tremelio and Bremo. Despite all appearances, Envy is in on the gag; this is why he emphasizes his *forbearance*, and his intent to *bear* with her. The audience may not realize it yet, but he is making some pretty clever puns which are echoed at several points throughout the play: "Beare thou the head of this most monstrous Beast" (B2r); "the Beare that thou didst see, / Did she not beare a bucket on her arme?" (B2v). While Comedy's warlike invocations may seem somewhat strange at first blush, they are entirely appropriate to a play that prizes chivalric action and derives some of its biggest laughs from scenes of violence and death. I would suggest that much of the play's peculiar energy is generated from the clash of comic and tragic signifiers, the portentous inflation and comic deflation of its characters, and its abrupt transitions from bloody slaughter to pastoral lovemaking to the comic business – and theatrical expediency – of removing bodies from the stage. Both Comedy and Envy purport to motivate the action, and in the case of Envy's treble duty in the cast list, he is quite literally seen to do so, dropping in whenever the hero needs a new monster to slay. Robert Y. Turner describes the phenomenon of causal inductions as being in some ways a hangover from the morality plays and a medieval-allegorical habit of mind.[12] Arvin Jupin, in his Garland edition of *Mucedorus*, suggests that the play's logical discontinuities and inconsistencies in motivation may be explained away as symptoms of the overriding causal influence of Envy or Comedy.[13] I would argue that their intervention is not only fundamental to the dramaturgy, but one of its cleverest features: while Comedy and Tragedy pretend to be fighting it out on a cosmic level with their mortal instruments, they are in fact merely telling a conventional romance story. Moreover, the story told is one lifted, in part, from the Musidorus plotline of Sidney's *Arcadia*. Whenever we perceive the intervention of Comedy or Tragedy in this play, it is within and according to the dictates of romance convention. By dramatizing an allegory of the arbitrary imposition of genre on narrative and ultimately making this contrivance serve as the means through which the artificial conventions of its own genre are realized, *Mucedorus* may be seen to self-reflexively interrogate the terms of its own construction, showing off its implausibilities and incongruities while, paradoxically, granting them a kind of formal symmetry. As sophisticated and productive as *Mucedorus'* use of its framing device may be, it bears noting that *The Rare Triumphs of Love and Fortune* – upon which Shakespeare would draw as a source for his continued experimentation with tragicomic romance in *Cymbeline* – likewise contains a framing device which structures and purports to motivate the action of its main plot.

Rare Triumphs opens with a dumbshow in which a Fury, Tisiphone, incites discord amongst the Olympian gods. It is shortly revealed that the cause of this strife is rooted in a contention between Venus and Fortune. Venus, apparently, has been up to no good and "Blabs it abroad and beareth all the world in hand, / She must be thought the only Goddess of the world, / Exalting and suppressing whom she likes best, / Defacing altogether Lady Fortune's grace."[14] Fortune, claiming her due, demands that her power, which "changeth and supplanteth realms in twinkling of an hour" (A4r), be recognized. After a parade of dumbshows featuring archetypal victims of love and fortune – Dido and Aeneas, Pompey and Caesar, Hero and Leander, and Troilus and Cressida – yields inconclusive evidence of either's supremacy, Jupiter suggests that the goddesses prove their sovereignty by manipulating the fates of the young lovers of the main plot:

> Venus, for that they love thy sweet delight,
> Thou shalt [endevor] to encrease their ioy;
> And, Fortune, thou to manifest thy might,
> Their pleasures and their pastimes shalt destroye
> Ouerthwarting them with newes of freshe anoye;
> And she that most can please them or dispight,
> I will confirme to be of greatest might (B1v).

Characterized as such, Venus and Fortune come to personify the genres of comedy and tragedy, respectively. As the main plot unfolds, the close of each act is punctuated by a short pageant in which either Comedy or Tragedy – according to the present fortunes of the protagonists – crosses the stage accompanied by noise from appropriate instruments – viols for Venus, drum and trumpets for Fortune – and declares herself in the ascendant. What Samuel Johnson would call "the absurdity of the conduct"[15] – the fantastical implausibility of the play's events and the seemingly unmotivated actions of the characters – is underscored by the seemingly arbitrary triumphs of Comedy and Tragedy. At the play's end, when it appears that tragedy will prevail, Jupiter steps in and calls it a draw. Both Tragedy and Comedy have demonstrated their equal might, and so he brings the action to a close with the decision that Fortune in this instance should subordinate her will to Love since it was her efforts that threatened to frustrate the *natural* outcome of the protagonists' affair. Venus is reconciled to Fortune and it is decreed that henceforth,

> ….whomsoever one of you prefer,
> The other shall be subject unto her…
> By proper course, each one in his discent
> Over mortall men and worldly things to raine
> By enterchange (G1r).

What is hinted at in the series of dumbshows in the first act but suppressed by Jupiter's casting Venus and Fortune in the roles of Comedy and Tragedy, is revealed in the Olympian reconciliation that incites and doubles the reconciliation of the main plot. That is, Love and Fortune often have shared aims in drama and can tend toward either comedy or tragedy in any given instant and at the wave of a sceptre or, more appropriately, with the stroke of a pen. Comedy and Tragedy are thus revealed to be more or less structurally identical – the outcome of an action, be it happy or tragic, is merely an arbitrary matter of "whomsoever one of you prefer." *Rare Triumphs*' and *Mucedorus*' personified dramatizations of genre as an external force that artificially imposes itself on the action of a play, facilitating its intelligibility while mediating the audience's response by quite literally framing their perspective on what transpires, are remarkable enough in themselves. But what makes their dramaturgies truly innovative and sets their frame devices apart from the embodied psychomachias of the morality tradition is their self-conscious subordination of the fiction of the Venus-Fortune/Envy-Comedy contentions to the demands of the modal substructure–romance–that has *really* been motivating the plot all along. In *Rare Triumphs*, when the frame dissolves into the main action and Venus reveals the true identities of Bomelio and Hermione to the awe-struck mortals, we see that it belonged to the play's structure from the outset that the story would, or at least should, end happily. The seeds of the revelation, after all, have been planted at the beginning, and the tone throughout is comic. Any hint of Olympian *gravitas*, generated by the stately, clunky diction of the contending gods or by the edifying series of dumbshows is effectively skewered by the parodic commentary of Vulcan. Comedy, it is implied, is the preferred tonal mode for romance narratives. As much as Venus and Fortune may pretend to control the genre and thereby the action of the play, they are inevitably a part of a larger fiction which operates according to the conventions of romance. With Jupiter's acknowledgment that a happy reconciliation is the natural outcome for Hermione and Fidelia – and as such, frustrated only by Fortune's exertions – the *deus ex machina* or providential scheme is made to intervene on its own behalf, and ultimately in the service of a higher power: that is, the "natural outcome," or appropriateness of the happy ending to romance. Both *Mucedorus* and *Rare Triumphs* play with the conventions of the causal induction, in order to explore the nature of the genres and modes with which they identify. In summary, I would argue that in both texts, the interplay between the induction and main action lays out a very rough blueprint for a native form of tragicomedy, steeped in the motifs of English romance, that eschews Guarini's prescriptions and embraces mirth and killing–not unlike the way that *Cymbeline* and *Pericles* trouble their overall comic actions with deaths, intrigues, and potentially tragic complications. It is tempting to speculate that *Mucedorus'* success may well have recommended its brand of 'tragicomic' romance to Shakespeare as a sophisticated yet inoffensive alternative to the tragicomic dramaturgies of the boys' companies.

The bare fact that the King's Men performed *Mucedorus* at court in 1610 suggests their confidence in the play's subject matter and its admittedly old-fashioned dramaturgy and verse style. Although they saw fit to emend it, for the most part their additions leave the original intact. This suggests that however quaint, deficient, or old-fashioned the text may have seemed in 1610, it was also thought sufficiently supple and adaptive to a contemporary playing style and tone. I suspect that some measure of the play's durability is owing to its internal instability, its simultaneous tendency toward self-parody and affirmation of the the conventions that it addresses. Mucedorus' inability to account for why he was delayed from his rendezvous with Amadine at the well, for instance, points up an apparent failing in plotting, while acknowledging the conventional and theatrical necessity that he be detained. Similarly, Mouse's irreverent and skeptical running commentary has a deflationary effect on many of the chivalric pretensions of the play's characters, and in this respect bears a strong resemblance to the wily clown-servant Subtle Shift from *Sir Clyomon and Sir Clamydes* which also served as a source for *Cymbeline*. Furthermore, the heavily alliterative verse style of the early dramatic romances, exemplified in Clamydes' opening line "As to the wearie wandring wights, whom waltring waves environ,"[16] and such motifs as "hugie heaps of care" (A2v) are echoed and gently lampooned in lines like Segasto's in *Mucedorus*: "When heaps of harmes do hover over head" (B2r). *Mucedorus'* embrace of romance does not preclude self-parody, and its playful capacity for poking fun at its own "naïve" conventions further serves to distance it from the Children of the Queen's Revels' repertory. Whereas the prologue to the Queen's Revels' play *The Isle of Gulls* also satirizes the popular taste for "stately pend historie, as thus, / *The rugged windes, with rude and ragged ruffes. &c.*," its main action offers a very different and fractious alternative to the pleasant matter of *Mucedorus*.[17]

Furthermore, the additions to Q3 *Mucedorus* seem primarily intended to enlarge upon theatrically proven aspects of the play. The popularity of Mouse's antics is attested to by their advertisement on the title pages of the extant quartos, and the King's Men appear to have responded to this phenomenon by giving him an extra scene with the bear: two theatrical birds of opportunity killed with one stone. They also interpolated a modified ending and a scene in which Mucedorus' father laments his son's disappearance, which momentarily heightens the play's tragic potential and in turn facilitates a stronger emotional climax at the two families' reunion. Perhaps the most significant of the King's Men's additions is also the lengthiest, and it occurs immediately following the induction. Rather than beginning with the bear's attack, Segasto's flight, and the shepherd's heroic intervention, we are presented with an expository scene that motivates Mucedorus' quest and establishes his royal birth, effectively spoiling what is perhaps the play's best joke – when the shepherd, without dramatic preparation or explanation reveals his true identity. This move makes the play seem less haphazard in construction while divesting Comedy and Envy of some of the causal influence they claim to exert upon the action, grounding the sometimes arbitrary motions of the plot in a more recognizable narrative. Mucedorus' journey is marked as a chivalrous quest when his intentions are established; he heard there was a pretty girl in Aragon and wants to see her for himself. Indeed, the opening scene tolls romance as clearly as Spenser's gentle knight "pricking on the plain," and is as crowded with romance conventions as may be. So thick are the motifs that already one suspects a gently parodic intent on the part of the playwright. Mucedorus' dialogue with Anselmo reveals the play's investment in a host of romance themes: filial and sovereign loyalty, intense male friendship, questing, magic, courtly love, botany as social metaphor, and fanciful disguise. Although the scene motivates the quest, it coyly refuses to offer a compelling explanation for Mucedorus' disguise. When Anselmo points out that a disguise is unnecessary and counterproductive–"what you rightly are will more commaund / Than best usurped shape" (A4v), Mucedorus is implacable and refuses the suggestion that he dress as a Florentine or mountebank. He slyly implies that the disguises of choice for Italianate and city comedies are old hat. Anselmo strikes gold when he suggests the shepherd's cassock – a costume from one Lord Julio's masque: surely the height of Jacobean courtly fashion in 1610. Pastoral and romance are all the rage, apparently, retroactively cool; Florentines are *so* last season, and what was old (*Mucedorus*, the play, for instance) is new again. This functions at once as an acknowledgment and an assertion of pastoral romance's ascendancy and as such heightens our sense of the play's self-conscious theatricality. In addition, Mucedorus' defence of his costume choice rests on precedent, convention, and fashion: he offers no further logical explanation as to why disguising himself is an appropriate decision. His seemingly arbitrary choice suggests that it is circumscribed by the convention that questing nobles disguise themselves in pursuit of their goal and that it is enough that he is acting in accordance with theatrical fashion and to the dictates of the genre which he, as the errant prince, embodies: "Better than Kinges have not disdain'd that state, / And much inferiour to obtaine their mate" (A4v). What this exchange amounts to is an overt metatheatrical wink to the audience, a wink that acknowledges the absurdity of the convention while embracing it wholeheartedly.

I contend that the romance tradition that *Mucedorus* and plays like it drew upon afforded Shakespeare a vast trove of conventions, themes, and narrative tropes that were already familiar to his audience and afforded him a flexible theatrical vocabulary in which to parse his experiments in tragicomedy. Romance, already so artificial, generically absorptive, self-conscious of its tropes and steeped in an awareness of its delights and absurdities, lent itself particularly well to a marriage between old, familiar forms and the new dramaturgies developing on the London scene. That romance tends to imagine its action as essentially tragicomic was equally fortuitous. That basic formula is perhaps most succinctly expressed by Shakespeare's Jove in *Cymbeline*, explaining the workings of destiny: "Whom best I love I cross; to make my gift, / The more delay'd, delighted."[18] I suggest that Shakespeare found a ready-made alternative dramaturgical and generic framework in the "mungrell Tragy-comedie" of romance drama that afforded him latitude to include both mirth and killing, high-feeling sentiment and bawdry in his plays, unrestricted by the rules of decorum that characterize Guarini's tragicomic formula.[19]

When Shakespeare wrote *Cymbeline* around 1609, he was thinking actively and critically about *The Rare Triumphs of Love and Fortune* and *Clyomon and Clamydes*, published, intriguingly, in 1599, the year after *Mucedorus*' first extant edition. These plays come from the same romantic tradition that *Mucedorus* revels in. That tradition would provide the narrative and theatrical vocabulary for a reimagining of romance in the new kind of tragicomedy Shakespeare would continue to experiment with in *The Winter's Tale*, *The Tempest*, *Henry VIII*, and *The Two Noble Kinsmen*. *Mucedorus* may well be a missing link; the play whose success in print, and whose hypothetical performance between 1604-6 may have proved that some of the matter and some of the dramaturgical methods of the old romance plays of the 1570s and '80s were due for a modified return.

Notes

1. See Jonathan Bate and Eric Rasmussen, *William Shakespeare and Others: Collaborative Plays* (New York: Palgrave MacMillan, 2013).

2. See Chapter eight of Edward Dowden's *Shakspere: A Critical Study of His Mind and Art* (London: Henry S. King & Co., 1875).

3. John Fletcher, *The faithfull shepheardesse*, (London: Edward Allde, 1610), (STC 11068), http://gateway.proquest.com.myaccess.library.utoronto.ca/openurl?ctx_ver=Z39.88-2003&res_id=xri:eebo&rft_id=xri:eebo:citation:99841346. A2v.

4. Philip Sidney, *An apologie for poetrie. VVritten by the right noble, vertuous, and learned, Sir Phillip Sidney, Knight*, (London: James Roberts, 1595), (STC 22534), http://gateway.proquest.com.myaccess.library.utoronto.ca/openurl?ctx_ver=Z39.88-2003&res_id=xri:eebo&rft_id=xri:eebo:citation:99846470. K2r.

5. Lucy Munro, *Children of the Queen's Revels: A Jacobean Theatre Repertory*, (New York: Cambridge University Press, 2011), p. 96.

6. Munro, *Children of the Queen's Revels*, p. 98.

7. Gurr, Andrew, *Playgoing in Shakespeare's London*, (Cambridge: Cambridge University Press, 2008), p. 120.

8. Philip Sidney, *An apologie for poetrie*. K1r.

9. Anon., A most pleasant comedie of Mucedorus the Kings sonne of Valentia, and Amadine the Kinges daughter of Aragon With the merry conceites of Mouse. Amplified with new additions, as it was acted before the Kings Maiestie at White-hall on Shrouesunday night. By his Highnes Seruantes vsually playing at the Globe. Very delectable, and full of coneeited [sic] mirth. (London: William White, 1610), (STC 2nd ed. / 18232), http://gateway.proquest.com.myaccess.library.utoronto.ca/openurl?ctx_ver=Z39.88-2003&res_id=xri:eebo&rft_id=xri:eebo:citation:99842093. F3r.

10. Richard T. Thornberry, "A Seventeenth-Century Revival of *Mucedorus* in London Before 1610," *Shakespeare Quarterly* 28.3 (1977), 362-4.

11. Anon., A most pleasant comedie of Mucedorus. A3r.

12. See Robert Y. Turner, "The Causal Induction in Some Elizabethan Plays", *Studies in Philology* 60.2 (1963): 183-90

13. Arpin Jupin, *A Contextual Study and Modern Spelling Edition of Mucedorus*. (New York: Garland, 1987).

14. Anon., *The rare triumphes of loue and fortune Plaide before the Queenes most excellent Maiestie: wherin are manye fine conceites with great delight*. (London: E.A., 1589), (STC 24286), http://gateway.proquest.com.myaccess.library.utoronto.ca/openurl?ctx_ver=Z39.88-2003&res_id=xri:eebo&rft_id=xri:eebo:citation:99846788. A2v.

15. Richard Danson Brown and David Johnson, *Shakespeare 1609: Cymbeline and the Sonnets* (New York: St. Martin's Press, 2000), p. 6.

16. Anon., *The historie of the tvvo valiant knights, Syr Clyomon Knight of the Golden Sheeld, sonne to the King of Denmarke: and Clamydes the white Knight, sonne to the King of Suauia As it hath bene sundry times acted by her Maiesties Players*. (London: Thomas Creede, 1599). (STC 5450A), http://gateway.proquest.com.myaccess.library.utoronto.ca/openurl?ctx_ver=Z39.88-2003&res_id=xri:eebo&rft_id=xri:eebo:citation:99845937. A3r.

17. John Day, *The ile of guls. As it hath been often playd in the blacke Fryars, by the Children of the Reuels*, (London: John Trundle, 1606), http://gateway.proquest.com.myaccess.library.utoronto.ca/openurl?ctx_ver=Z39.88-2003&res_id=xri:eebo&rft_id=xri:eebo:citation:99840846. A2v.

18. William Shakespeare, *The Oxford Shakespeare: Cymbeline*, ed. Roger Warren (Oxford: Clarendon Press), 1998), 5.4.101-2.

19. Philip Sidney, *An apologie for poetrie*. K2r.

"The Actors of the Playe were Countreymen": the disastrous performance of *Mucedorus* in 1653

Alexandra F. Johnston[1]

One of the most pervasive myths in our understanding of the history of the English stage is that when the London city council closed the professional theatres within their jurisdiction in 1642, all of England "went dark." The work of Records of Early English drama project is disproving this assumption by the discovery of evidence all over the country of survivals of mimetic customs in towns and parishes (often hotly contested) and of scripted plays in private houses. One of the most interesting and revealing pieces of evidence is a pamphlet written by a Puritan divine in 1653 describing the performance of the highly popular Elizabethan romantic comedy first performed in 1590, *Mucedorus*. The pamphlet describes the performance of the play in the small Oxfordshire market town of Witney by a group of players from a nearby parish and makes clear not only the continuing popularity of the romance form, but the familiarity of the audience with the conventions of dramatic performance eleven years after the supposed suppression of playing.

The author of the pamphlet was John Rowe, a fellow of Corpus Christi College, Oxford, and a patristic scholar, appointed to be "lecturer" in the town of Witney by the then dominant Puritans. The title *Tragi-Comoedia* includes a brief description of the contents:

> Being a Brief Relation of the strange, and Wonderful hand of God discovered at Witney, in the *Comedy* Acted there February the third, where there were some *Slaine*, many *Hurt*, with severall other *Remarkable* Passages. Together with what was Preached in three Sermons on that occasion from *Rom.* I.18. Both which May serve as some Check to the Growing *Atheisme* of the Present Age"[2].

Rowe was born in Crediton, Devon in 1626. Admitted as battler to New Hall Inn, Oxford in 1642, he was displanted along with the rest of his college by the arrival of the Royal Mint with the Court in 1643. He continued his education in a more congenial atmosphere at the Puritan stronghold of Emmanuel College, Cambridge, from which he graduated with his B.A. in 1646. Two years later a changed Oxford recognized his degree and on 12 December 1648 he received his M.A. from his original university. The next year he was made a fellow of Corpus Christi by the parliamentary visitors. Besides his interest in patristics, he was as well read in philosophy and jurisprudence as the schoolmen, and was remarkable for keeping a diary in Greek all his life. The lectureship in Witney was his first preferment while he retained his fellowship in Corpus. After his time in Oxfordshire, he returned briefly to Devon where he was lecturer in Tiverton. In 1654 he became preacher in Westminster Abbey and pastor of an independent congregation that met in the Abbey. His high standing in the eyes of the Commonwealth government is reflected in his appointment in 1660 as one of the approvers of ministers. At the Restoration he lost all his offices, although he remained pastor of his independent congregation, taking it first to Bartholomew Close and afterwards to Holborn. He died in 1677.[3]

He was, then, still in his twenties when the events of February 3, 1652 took place – a young and zealous fellow of Corpus Christi, "tall and dignified with a pleasing manner,"[4] as the *DNB* tells us, dividing his time between Oxford and the small market town of Witney thirteen miles away. The pamphlet was published in Oxford by the printer Lichfield and it is part of the complex body of polemical material against things "ungodly" published during the Commonwealth (1649-1660) after the beheading of King Charles I and before the Restoration of his son King Charles II.[5]

In his second section entitled "A breife narrative of the play acted at *Whitny* the third of February 1652. Together with its sad and Tragicall End," Rowe describes the preparation for and subsequent performance of *Mucedorus* in Witney. Few scholars have picked up the reference.[6] Chambers remarks the performance with a dismissive sentence, "After the suppression of the theatres in 1642, *Mucedorus* was acted by strolling players in various parts of Oxfordshire," a phraseology that is picked up in the introductions of modern editions of the play.[7] Some years ago, as I was gathering material for the Oxfordshire collection in the Records of Early English Drama series, I read the pamphlet and was struck both by what it can tell us about local dramatic activity and by its coherence and fairness as a piece of polemic writing. Rowe may have considered plays ungodly but he does not condemn the players and, in his careful journalistic approach to the event, he has tried to be as factual as possible. This concern for fact has provided us with an unexpected and detailed account of a parish performance that persisted into the Commonwealth period.

The February performance of *Mucedorus* ended in disaster. It was played on the second floor of a former brewhouse turned pub in Witney and the floor tipped at line 32 of Act IV Scene ii during the scene between Bremo and Amadine. Bremo had just begun his speech,

> Thou shalt be fed with quailes and partridges
> With blacke birds, larkes, thrushes and nightingales

> Thy drinke shall bee goates milke and christal water,
> Distilled from the fountains & the clearest springs.
> And all the dainties that the woods afforde,
> Ile freely give thee to obtain thy loue (32-7)[8]

The actors and many of the audience were shot down into the floor below, into a space still full of the detritus from the days when the building was a brewhouse.

Rowe describes the event and then tallies the dead and injured,

> The fall was not very quick, but somewhat slow, & gentle, in so much that some that were present thought it was part of the play, (but it proved the saddest part) & expected when they should be taken up againe, yet was it not so slowe as that they were able to recover themselves, for the actors then in the action fell down, and a great number of people with them into the under roome ... There were five slaine outright, wherof three were Boys, two of which being about seaven, or eight yeares old or thereabout; the other neer twelve: the other two were Girles, the elder of which being fourteen, or fiveteen, and the younger twelve or thirteen yeares old. A woman also had her legg sorely broken that the surgeons were forced to cut it off, and she dyed within three or four dayes after it was cut off. Many were hurt, and sorely bruised, to the number of about threescore, that we have certaine information of, besides those that conceale their griefes ...[9]

But how did a play come to be performed in the midst of the Interregnum in a provincial town and what caused the unfortunate disaster?

The players came from the parish of Stanton Harcourt, a tiny village about four miles south east of Witney. Stanton Harcourt was part of the manor of an ancient, but by this time, impoverished, Norman family called de Harcourt. The manor house is still owned by the descendants of the family and, of course, the family had held the advowson of the parish church before the Reformation. This meant that the relationship between the family and the church was particularly close. The church and the walled manor house still stand side by side down a small cul de sac off the main street of the modern village. The Harcourt most likely to have a tangential part in this story is Robert Harcourt (1574/5 – 1631), an "adventurer and author" according to the *DNB*.[10] Robert's second wife was the grand-daughter of John de Vere, fifteenth earl of Oxford and so a cousin of the seventeenth earl of Oxford, the Shakespeare pretender. The de Vere connection brought Robert to the attention of the court and, in 1609, he received the patronage of Prince Henry for an expedition to Guiana in South America.

By 1609, scholars generally agree that *Mucedorus* was owned by the King's Men. The title page of the 1610 edition tells us that is has been "Amplified with new additions, as it was acted before the Kings Maiestie at Whitehall on Shrove-Sunday night *By his hynes Seruantes usually playing to the Globe.*" Although not certain, Arvin Jupin agrees with Fitzroy Pile that Shrove Sunday 1609 is the most likely date for the performance at court. Shrove Sunday in 1609 was 26 February. Robert Harcourt sailed for Guiana in April 1609. It is perfectly possible that he attended the performance at court. Although the text that was used for the Witney performance contains the additions from the 1610 edition, as we will see, Harcourt could well have obtained a copy after his return from South America and taken it home to Stanton Harcourt.

We have some evidence that the purchase of play-texts was one of the things country gentlemen did when they went up to London. For example, Sir Thomas Temple of Stowe in Buckinghamshire visited London in 1600-01. His steward, Raphe Handes, recorded the following expenses for that trip,

Item your standing at Paules Sermon	iiij d
...	
Item your place at Paules Sermon againe	iiij d
Item paid in part for your standing at the Tylt	xij d
Item for the Conquest of west India	xx d
Item deliuered y<.> at the plaie at Paules	xv d[11]

The Conquest of the West Indies by John Day, William Haughton, and Wentworth Smith (now lost) was registered by the Admiral's Men that year.[12]

Although we have no conclusive evidence that the text used in 1653 *was* the 1610 edition, Robert Harcourt or his son Simon (who took over the manor of Stanton Harcourt in 1635) could also have bought the play in a later edition remembering Robert's association with the court in 1609. However, it is likely that it was the 1610 edition since John Rowe tells us that this was not the first time the "countreymen" of Stanton Harcourt had performed the play. In his first paragraph he writes, "This *Play* was an old *Play*, and had been Acted by some of *Stanton-Harcourt* men many years since"(198). In any case, in the fall of 1652, the parishioners of Stanton Harcourt conceived the idea of a fundraiser – for that is clearly what this production was meant to be – and someone remembered the success of their earlier production of *Mucedorus*. When the idea was broached to perform the play it must have seemed attractive to the new generation of players since the title page carries the assurance "ten persons may easily play it."[13] Chambers was right to suggest that the Witney performance was done by "strolling players," but this was not a professional troupe but players who had a very local base in the parish of Stanton Harcourt.

Rowe's interviews have given us a picture of parish dramatic activity that is startlingly like the parish dramatic activity of over a century before, where groups of entertainers from parishes in the Thames Valley would visit neighbouring parishes in order to raise money for the upkeep of their church.[14] The ancient tradition where the priest was responsible for the upkeep and appointments of all parts of the church east of the rood screen, while the parish was responsible for the upkeep of the rest of the building and the property, continued to place a heavy financial burden on the laity. The parishioners of Stanton Harcourt were simply continuing an ancient and honourable custom. The major difference between the playmaking recorded here and the historic situation seems to be the nature of the entertainment. The earlier evidence indicates that parish folk plays, Biblical plays or morris dancers were shared with neighbouring parishes. Here we have a more ambitious project, the production of a romance that had once been played by professional players in London.

Work on the play, Rowe tells us, began at Michaelmas in late September with weekly rehearsals (198). By Christmas, the show was ready to go up and was performed first in Stanton Harcourt itself and then in the neighbouring parishes of Standlake and Northmoor (each less than two miles away), South Leigh slightly over two miles to the northwest and then Cumnor over three miles to the southeast. By the end of January, the players felt ready for the larger venue of Witney just beyond South Leigh.

The town of Witney had a history of dramatic performance and festival. Its parish church, dedicated to St Mary the Virgin, was one of the few in the country that celebrated Easter with a puppet play version of the resurrection. Lambarde's late sixteenth-century *Dictionarium* has the following entry with its own anti-Catholic bent:

> In the Dayes of ceremonial Religion they used at Wytney to set foorthe yearly in the maner of a Shew, or Enterlude, the Resurrection of our Lord and Saviour *Chryste*, partly of Purpose to draw thyther some Concourse of People that might spend their Money in the Towne, but cheiflie to allure by pleasant Spectacle the comon Sort to the Likinge of Popishe Maumetrie; for the which Purpose, and the more lyvely thearby to exhibite to the Eye the hole Action of the Resurrection, the Preistes garnished out certein smalle Puppets, representinge the Parsons of *Christe,* the Watchmen, *Marie,* and others, amongest the which one bare the Parte of a wakinge Watcheman, who (espiinge *Christ* to arise) made a continual Noyce, like to the Sound that is caused by the Metinge of two Styckes, and was therof comonly called *Jack Snacker of Wytney.*[15]

Witney also held summer festivals in support of the parish. We have only traces of evidence for the event in the fragmentary churchwardens' accounts where receipts for "whitsontide sport*es*" are recorded for 1610, 1620 and 1628.[16] More details about the possible nature of the summer event comes from a Civil War document, *The King Found at Southwell.*[17] It was printed in London in 1646 for a Mr. F. Loyd, a student of Christ Church and Captain of the Christ Church garrison, and presented to the Duke of York. The garrison, left stationed in Oxford in the middle of the Civil War, decided to leave the town for some "rest and recreation" and had arranged to be met in Witney by morris dancers – a troop that included Maid Marion and two fools, one of whom tumbled for the visitors – country fiddlers, a taborer, a pair of bagpipes, a harper and a group of singers. The pamphlet is, in effect, a description of the day's revelries in which the student soldiers danced, joined with the entertainers in various capers, and got very drunk. That such an array of entertainers could be summoned to be present in a town like Witney in 1646 argues the continuing tradition of folk customs in this very conservative corner of Oxfordshire. In choosing to come to Witney with their production of *Mucedorus*, then, the men of Stanton Harcourt could be reasonably assured of a receptive audience.

By the time the players arrived in Witney to ask permission of the Bailiffs to perform in the town, at least seven performances had taken place within less than six weeks in a very small district. The prospective audience must have been aware of the production. This may explain the astonishing number of people Rowe records as attending the performance – between three and four hundred. The fact that it was a market day may also have contributed to the large audience of men, women and children who crowded together at seven o'clock on a dark February evening summoned by drums and trumpets to begin the evening with dancing. Rowe even provides a sketch of the brewhouse turned pub. The weight of the crowd and the vigour of the dance may well have contributed to the disaster. The shorter beam spanning the width of the room was not fastened into the walls but rested "upon a shoulder of stone." Once it broke in the middle, there was no residual strength as there would have been had the beam been securely fastened into the side walls. The break removed all vestige of horizontal support from the floor, and allowed the fatal tipping that shot so many of the people into the lower room. It could be said that the disaster was caused not by the hand of God but by the size and robustness of the audience.

Rowe did not attend the play. He and his like-minded Puritan companions had spent the evening in nearby Oxford at a prayer meeting that, for them, would have been a more suitable preparation for the impending Lenten season than the ancient, more festive, Shrovetide custom of a play. He and his friends arrived back in Witney shortly after the disaster when they pitched in to help. His account of the affair is the result of his journalistic interest in getting the story right.

He begins by recounting what he had been told about the rehearsals and the performances in neighbouring villages, and then brings the narrative to the point when the players arrived in Witney:

> The last place they came at was *Witny*, where it pleased the Lord to discover his displeasure, against such wicked and ungodly *Playes* by an eminent hand. Some few dayes before the *Play* was to be Acted, one of *Stanton* came to the *Baylife* of *Witny* telling him *that there were some Countrey men that had learn'd to make a Play, and desired his Leave to shew it*, his aime being (as the *Baylife* conceiv'd) that they might have the Liberty of the *Towne-Hall*. Leave also was desired of the other *Baylife*, but they being denied by both *Baylifs*, they pitched on the *White Hart*, a chiefe Inne of the Towne to Act their *Play* there. The day when it was Acted, was the third of *Fe- | bruary*, the same day when many Godly People, Townesmen and Schollars of *Oxford*, kept a Solemne Day of *Fast* at *Carfax*.[18] About seaven a Clock at Night they caused a Drum to beat, and a Trumpet to be sounded to gather the People together. The people flocked in great multitudes, Men, Women, and Children, to the number (as is guess'd) of three Hundred, some say foure hundred, and the Chamber where the *Play* was Acted being full, others in the Yard pressed sorely to get in. The people which were in the Roome were exceeding Joviall, and merry before the *Play* began, Young men and Maides dancing together, and so merry and frolick were many of the Spectators, that the Players could hardly get Liberty that they themselves might Act, but

at last a little Liberty being obtained, the *Play* it self began. In the beginning of it Enters a Person that took the name of Comedie, and speaks as follows...(198-9)

Rowe then proceeds to pick out the lines of Envy in the debate with Comedy to press home the uncomfortable truth that for the Witney production, Comedy did not win the contest. In Rowe's conceit, Envy's words in the prologue foretold the disaster that was to befall. Rowe must have had the text beside him as he wrote because he quotes the following lines from Envy's speeches accurately,

> Nay stay Minion stay there lyes a block;
> What all on mirth? I'le interrupt your tale,
> And mix your Musick with a Tragick end. (I i 8-10)
> ...
> Harken thou shalt heare noyse
> Shall fill the ayre with shrilling sound,
> And thunder Musicke to the Gods above   (24-6)
> ...
> In this brave Musick Envy takes delight
> Where I may see them wallow in their bloud,
> To spurne at Armes & Leggs quite shivered off,
> And heare the cryes of many thousand slaine. (30-33)
> ...
> – Trebble death shall crosse thee with dispight
> And make thee mourn where most thou joyest,
> Turning thy mirth into a deadly dole;
> Whirling thy pleasures with a peale of death,
> And drench thy methods in a Sea of bloud.   (55-9)

Rowe concludes this reading of the first scene with the ominous sentence, "Which passages if the Reader carry along with him, he will see how farre they were made good by the Divine hand, both on the Actors and the Spectators." He also uses lines 56 and 57 – "And makes thee mourn where most thou joyest" and "Turning thy mirthe into a deadly dole" – as headings for his final paragraphs where he asserts the presence of the hand of God in the disaster.

The prologue is in all the editions, but, from 1610 on, it is followed by a scene between Mucedorus and Anselmo where it is made clear that Mucedorus is the King's son. Anselmo gives him a cloak as a disguise and then there is a short new scene of Mouse running from the bear which is interpolated after the Mucedorus/Anselmo scene and the second scene in the first editions where Segasto and Amadine entered pursued by the bear:

> *Enter Mouse with a Bottle of Hay*

> Mouse O horrible, terrible! Was euer poore Gentleman so scard out of his seauen Senses? A Beare? Nay sure it can not be a Beare, but some Deuill in a Beares Doublet: for a Beare could neuer haue had that agilitie, to haue frighted me. Well, Ile see my Father hang'd, before Ile serue his Horse any more: Well Ile carry home my Bottle of Hay, and for once, make my Fathers Horse turn Puritane and obserue Fasting-dayes, for he gets not a bit. But soft, this way she followed me, therefore Ile take the other Path, and because Ile be sure to haue an eye on him, I will takes the hands with some foolish Creditor, and make euery steppe backward.
>
> *As he goes backwards, the Beare comes in, and he tumbles ouer her, And runs away, and leaues his bottle of Hay behind him.*

Rowe took particular exception to this scene:

> The matter of the *Play* is scurrilous, impious, blasphemous in severall passages. One passage of it hath such a bitter Taunt against all *Godly persons* under the nature of *Puritans*, and at *Religion* it selfe, under the phrase *of observing Fasting days*, that it may not be omitted, it was almost in the beginning of the *Play*, and they were some of the Clownes words when he first began to Act, *Well Ile see my Father hang'd before Ile serve his Horse any more, well Ile carry home my bottle of Hay and for once make my Fathers Horse turne Puritan, and observe Fasting dayes, for he gets not a bitt*. How remarkable was this that some of them that were called *Puritans* in the dayes of old, had spent that | very day in *Oxford* in Fasting and Prayer; and that the Lord by so eminent an hand should testifie against such, who were not scoffers at *Godly persons*, but at *Religion* it selfe (200).

But having vented his displeasure he returns to his narrative,

> Thus had they continued their sport for an hour, and halfe, as some of the Spectators say, but as is more probable, about two houres, for they were ordinarily three houres in acting it (as the Players say) and there were aboute two parts in three of the play were passed over in this Action. At which time it pleased God to put a stop to their mirth, and by an immediate hand of his owne, in causing the chamber to sink, and fall | under them, to put an end to this ungodly Play before it was thought, or intended by them.
>
> The Actors who were now in action were *Bremo a wild man*, (courting, and solliciting his Lady, and among other things, begging a *Kisse* in this verse.
>
> > Come kisse me (Sweet) for all my favours past)

And *Amadine* the Kings daughter (as named in the Play) but in truth a young man attired in a womans Habit. The words which were then speaking were these, the words of *Bremo* to his Lady

> Thou shalt be fed with Quailes, and Partridges,
> With Black-birds, Larkes, Thrushes,
> and Nightingales.

> Various reports there have been concerning the words spoken at that time, as that it should be sayed, *the Devill was now come to act his part:* some People might say so, observing the *wild mans* carriage, and some other passages that went before, where there was mention made of the Divell in a Bares dublet, the *wild man* then acting the Bares part: and indeed we have it upon good information that there were such words spoken; only they were the *spectators* words and not the *Actors*: but this we are assured of, the words then spoken by the *Actor* were those above mentioned, as *he himselfe* acknowledged, and we find them printed so in the Book [i.e. the text that he had beside him] (200-01).

This confusion over what was said at the moment of crisis attests to the fact that Rowe was not there at the time. From what he reports it seems clear that Bremo doubled as the Bear. Nevertheless, the way he conveys the contradictory things he was told also conveys the terror and confusion of the moment. His description of what followed the disaster is a compelling one. He has captured the panic of the moment as well as the longterm pain of those who lost their children and other relatives. The immediate panic screams from this passage:

> One that was present was so much affrighted (as was said) that she thought her selfe verily to be in Hell, which we do the rather insert because whoever shall put the circumstances together may well say it was a little resemblance of that black, and dismall place, there being so ma | ny taken in the middest of their sinfull practises, and thrust into a pit together where they were left in darknesse, the *Lights* being put out by the fall, where the dust that was raised made a kind of Mist, and Smoake, where there were the most lamentable skreekes, and out-cryes that may be imagined; where they were shut up as in a prison, and could not get themselves out, (the doore of the under roome being blocked up, and their leg's being so pinioned, & wedged together by faggots, and other things, that fell down together with them from the upper roome, that they could not stirre to help themselves.) Another (as is said) supposing his limbs to be all plucked asunder cryed out, *that they should cut off his head*: this is certaine, the fright was exceeding great, and many were dead for a time that afterward came to themselves. When the people were come to themselves, there was a fearfull, and most lamentable cry, so*me* crying one thing, so*me* another, some crying *aid for the Lords sake, others crying Lord have mercy on us, Christ have mercy on us,* others cryed oh my Hus-

band! a second, oh my Wife! a third, Oh my child! and another said No body loves *me* so well as to see where my child is. Others cryed out for Ladders, and Hatchets to make their passage out, for the chamber falling, the doore of the under roome was so Blocked up that they could not get out there, so that they were fain to break the barres of the window, and most of the people got out that way though it were a good space of time before | they could get forth (202-03).

Nor does Rowe forget or vilify the players:

The other Players that were not in action were in the Attiring-roome which was joyning to the chamber that fell, and they helped to save some of the people which were neer that part. Those of the people that fell not down, but were preserved by that meanes got out at the window of the upper roome (203).

And the picture of the actor playing Bremo protecting the boy playing Amadine is particularly striking:

The man in womans apparrell lay panting for breath and had it not been for *Bremo* his fellow Actor, he had been stifled; but *Bremo* having recovered himselfe a little, bare up the others head with his arme, whereby he got some breath, and so was preserved; but both the one, and the other were hurt; *Bremo* being so sorely bruised, as that he was fain to keep his bed for two dayes after, and the Lady had her beauty mar'd, her face being swoln by the hurt taken in the fall (204).

However, some of the most interesting comments come at the end of the narrative when Rowe clearly went round the town interviewing those who had had the misfortune to be involved and recording their attitudes to the idea of attending another play. Some said they would never go to a play again while others said "they would go againe, if it were tomorrow next"(204). Clearly, the only thing unusual about this performance was the unstable condition of the playing space.

Eleven years after the closing of the professional theatres in London, playmaking in the countryside seems to have been a sufficiently common occurrence that the people of Witney and the surrounding countryside understood what the players were offering. They knew about romance plays and they also knew how the evening would progress beginning with the trumpet and drums to call the audience and to first enjoy the dance. Even after the Witney disaster, members of the audience could speak with confidence about future opportunities to see plays. The Puritan divines, such as Rowe, may have preached against the playmaking as an ungodly and blasphemous activity but it is clear that it continued. Like so much of the "received tradition" about the history of the English theatre, this piece of Puritan polemic must be re-thought in light of the contextual evidence provided by the extensive research of the Records of Early English Drama project. Rowe's pamphlet is as much evidence of a vigorous *continuing* practice of playmaking as it is of Puritan disapproval of the theatre. A man of stern convictions but also one of compassion and attention to detail, John Rowe has provided us with an account of a living tradition that did not die when the professional houses were closed but continued its long-established customary life deep in the English countryside.

Notes

1. Alexandra F. Johnston."'It pleased the Lord to discover his displeasure': the 1652 Performance of *Mucedorus* in Witney," *Leeds Studies in English*, N.S. 32 (2001), 195-210.

2. It was printed in Oxford by L. Lichfield, for Henry Cripps, Anno Dom. 1653. The Bodleian shelfmark for its copy of the pamphlet is Oxford, Bodleian Library, Gough Oxf 45(5). It can be found on WING Film 509 item R2067. I misdated the performance in my 2001 edition. Rowe used the common style of dating in England until the mid-eighteenth century that began the new year at the Feast of the Annunciation, March 25. By that reckoning it was 1652 but by modern reckoning it is 1653 – the same year that the pamphlet was printed. I am grateful to Joshua McEvilla for bringing this to my attention.

3. Stephen Wright, "Rowe, John (1626/7–1677)," *Oxford Dictionary of National Biography*, Oxford University Press, 2004; online ed., Jan 2008. See http://www.oxforddnb.com.myaccess.library.utoronto.ca/view/article/24201. Accessed 17 April 2015. See also *The Dictionary of National Biography*, The Compact Edition (Oxford: Oxford University Press, 1975), p. 1816.

4. Compact *DNB*, p. 1816. s.v. Rowe, John.

5. A notice of it appeared in *Severall Proceedings of State Affaires* in an issue printed "for Robert Ibbitson dwelling in Smithfield near Hosier Lane" dated 7 July 1653. Again I am grateful to Joshua McEvilla for the reference.

6. An American scholar, Thornton S. Graves, working at the same time as Chambers, published the text of the narrative with no commentary in his "Notes on Puritanism and the Stage" in *Studies in Philology* 18 (1921), 141-69. The only modern edition I could trace was a facsimile edition in the Garland series, *The English Stage: Attack and Defense 1577-1730*, Ed. Arthur Freeman, *Tragi-Comoedia* (New York: Dissertations-G, 1973) with a brief preface.

7. See, for example, R.A. Fraser and Norman Rabkin, eds., *Drama of the English Renaissance I: The Tudor Period* (New York: Macmillan, 1976), p. 463.

8. All quotations from the play are taken from Arvin H. Jupin, ed., *Mucedorus, a modern spelling edition* (New York: Garland, 1987).

9. All quotations from the pamphlet are from my edition in "It pleased the Lord;" this passage is p. 202

10. Joyce Lorimer, "Harcourt, Robert (1574/5–1631)," *Oxford Dictionary of National Biography* (Oxford: Oxford University Press, 2004); online ed., Oct 2009 http://www.oxforddnb.com.myaccess.library.utoronto.ca/view/article/12241. Accessed 17 April 2015.

11. Huntington Library, San Marino California, Stowe Collection: Temple Papers, SSTF Box 5.

12. Alfred Harbage, *Annals of English Drama*, 975-1700, Samuel Schoenbaum, rev. (Philadelphia: U. of Pennsylvania Press, 1964), pp. 78-9.

13. Fraser and Rabkin, *Drama of the English Renaissance I*, p. 464.

14. See Alexandra F. Johnston, "Summer Festivals in the Thames Valley Counties," in T. Petitt and L. Søndergaard eds. *Custom, Culture and Community in the later Middle Ages* (Odense: Odense University Press, 1994), 37-56, and Alexandra F. Johnston and Sally-Beth MacLean, "Reformation and resistance in the Thames/Severn parishes: the dramatic witness," in Katherine L. French, Gary Gibbs and Beat Kümin, eds. *The Parish in English Life 1400-1600* (Manchester, 1997), 178-200.

15. Cited in Pamela Sheingorn, *The Easter Sepulchre in England,* Early Drama, Art and Music Reference Series 5 (Kalamazoo: Medieval Institute Publications, 1987), pp. 294-5.
16. Oxfordshire Record Office, Ms DD Par Witney c.9, ff.34, 43, and 49v.
17. Its full title is *The King Found at Southwell, and the Oxford Gigg playd, and Sung at Witney Wakes: With the Masque shewed before divers Courtiers, and Cavaliers, that went thither from Oxford, and severall Ketches and Songs at the said Wakes.* The pamphlet is British Library E.336,14.
18. Carfax is the area in front of the parish church of St Martin in Oxford at the top of the High Street, the city center.

La farce du Poulier à six personnages
(The Farce of the Chicken Coop for Six Characters)
BnF Ms fr. 24341 (ff. 132ᵛ–144ᵛ)
Mario Longtin and Richard J. Moll

French farces are not usually associated with either courtly love or the medieval romance. Instead, the farce is considered a bawdy form which lacks complex narrative and literary sophistication. The comic tone of the genre, along with the stark brevity of most of the two hundred or so surviving plays, has often led medievalists and Renaissance specialists alike to treat farces as formulaic constructions. At its best, the farce could be a well-oiled machine which produced laughter. At its worse, the farce could lack the creativity and imagination necessary for a great dramatic text.[1] Not all farces, however, were written according to the same pattern or with the same thematic ends, and each and every witness of the genre needs to be scrutinized in order to better understand the great diversity of contexts and expression among medieval and Renaissance comedic drama. There is a world of difference, for example, between *La farce du Meunier de qui le diable emporte l'âme en enfer* (The Farce of the Miller Whose Soul is Carried to Hell by the Devil) of André de La Vigne and the farce of *Regnault qui se marie à La Vollée* (Regnault Who is Marrying On-the-Go): one is inserted inside a mystery play while the other stands alone as a wedding farce.[2] Many other farces reveal a close relationship between the courtly concerns of romance and the burlesque interests of fabliaux.

One such example, *La farce du Poulier à six personnages* (The Farce of the Chicken Coop for Six Characters),[3] challenges the received understanding of the genre. Most obviously, *La farce du Poulier*, at 732 lines, is far longer than is typical. The six actors necessary for performance, while not unheard of in French farce, are twice what is typical; most play-texts require only three or four actors. The material survival of the work is also unusual; there is no early printed copy, but the text is found, along with 73 other plays, in a manuscript from Rouen transcribed in the second half of the sixteenth century. The manuscript was produced by Jehan Le Hucher, who seems to have played an important part in the cultural world of Rouen.[4] Most farces survive only in early printed copies and, while manuscript copies are not unheard of, the sheer number of play-texts preserved in the "Rouen repertory" and the very late date of its production are striking.[5] Most of the plays in the manuscript, including *La farce du Poulier*, are not copies of earlier medieval works, but are products of Normandy in the sixteenth century. The plays, in other words, are clearly Renaissance productions, and this again challenges the common assumption that the farce is primarily a medieval genre. The manuscript itself is intricately linked to Rouen, the principal harbor and second city of France, and this also argues for a more context-driven approach to the genre rather than the *de facto* Parisian bias so often found in theater studies.[6]

The plot of *La farce du Poulier* revolves around the sexual gratification of two gentlemen and their wives who are "habillées en damoiselles" (dressed as ladies) (f. 132^v). Representatives of the gentry rarely occur in the farce, a genre more often peopled with labourers, merchants, farmers, priests and clerks. The other two characters, the Miller and his wife, are totally at home in this universe. *La farce du Poulier* exploits the interaction between these two distinct classes: the aristocratic owners of a mill and their wives on the one hand, and their tenants, the Miller and his wife, on the other. The Miller's wife, as is typical of the genre, is engaged in a sexual adventure, although she succeeds in deflecting the advances of her two noble suitors.[7] The gentlemen occasionally mimic the rhetoric of love from poetic tradition, with the second gentleman in particular referring to his would-be lover as "Mon tétin, m'amour, ma rose!" (My breast, my love, my rose!), but there is certainly no attempt to adopt the ideals of courtly love or any particular code of lovers. When not with the Miller's wife, their conversation is crude and lurid, and their attempts to buy her sexual favours turn love into a tawdry business transaction and the gentlemen themselves into would-be clients of a brothel.

But what is perhaps most striking in *La farce du Poulier* is the Miller's successful cuckolding of both gentlemen. As M. de la Hannetonière and M. de la Papillonnière[8] hide in the chicken coop, the Miller invites their willing wives to both his table and his bed, seducing the two ladies with coarse language and quick hands. The Miller's wife actively participates, as she is sent to fetch the ladies, literally becoming the *entremetteuse*, a panderer in the pursuit of her husband's sexual and financial desires.

Despite its many charms, *La farce du Poulier* is little known outside the circle of French theater specialists. As a complement to the articles found in this volume, we offer it here in French followed by an English verse translation. Since a modern critical edition in original French spelling already exists, and since a team of scholars is preparing a complete critical edition of all 74 play texts found in BnF fr. 24341, we opted to present the text here in modernized spelling. It is common practice to modernize the spelling of seventeenth-century French texts in order to make authors such as Corneille, Racine, LaFontaine and of course Molière, more accessible, especially in the classroom. This intrusive editorial practice is usually applied to texts from the classical period of French literature, but we decided to transgress the traditional divide of 1599 to allow a new readership access to this exceptional dramatic culture with as few obstacles as possible. A critical edition of *La farce du Poulier* does indeed present many obstacles, as the scribe of the manuscript, Jehan le Hucher, admits that he knows little "De l'orthograffe" (about spelling).[9] His texts, as a result, are very challenging even for specialists in the field. Actors, who are very rarely philologists or historians of the language, inevitably would waste valuable rehearsal time simply trying to work out the spelling and decipher the text. Given Le Hucher's honest assessment of his own weaknesses, and being interested in the dissemination of the material, we therefore feel that modernized spelling best serves the performance interests of the play.[10]

Editorial Principles

The modernized text remains faithful to the syllable count and rhyme scheme of the original. The placement of pronouns follows modern practice within lines: for example, *Je le vous donne* becomes *Je vous le donne*. Square brackets indicate a substantial modification to the original, which is explained in a following note. Parentheses indicate that a syllable is not pronounced and so is not counted in the octosyllabic line. English explanatory notes gloss obscure formulations or wording, but such notes are kept to a minimum since the translation/adaptation in English verse is meant to aid in the comprehension of the French text.

We have decided, for consistency, to set both the source text and the translation with the traditional French layout. The name of the character speaking (i.e. the speech prefix) is therefore printed above his or her speech rather than in the left margin. This layout was used in French medieval and Renaissance dramatic manuscripts, and it is the layout adopted by BnF Ms fr. 24341 for all the 74 play-texts it contains.

Translation

The English translation was initially completed as a supplement to a conference presentation. It was meant to serve as a literal gloss on the original French text, and as such it was produced in prose and had all the woodenness and choppiness which is typical of such productions. As the written project took shape, however, we realized that the literal, clunky, prose translation had little to do with issues of performance. We therefore undertook to transform the prose translation into a verse adaptation which would mimic our sense of the farce as it would appear on stage.

It is a medieval truism that all verse lies.[11] The demands of meter and rhyme quite often make it impossible to translate verse from one language to another while maintaining rigorous adherence to the meaning of the source text. We quickly decided, therefore, to produce a text which, to use another medieval construction, translated sense for sense, rather than word for word.[12] By *sense*, here, however, we mean both the sense of the original French text and the sense of the farce as a whole. The medieval or early modern writer of farce was able to create patterns of association, *double entendre* and outright bawdy puns through rhythm and rhyme, but such locutions are often impossible to replicate in the target language. And so, in those places where it has been unfeasible to reproduce everything from the source text in the translation, we have attempted to maintain the tone of the original, even if through different means. For example, "Le Meunier" flirts with "La Deuxième Damoiselle" by reminding her that, while she visited the mill, her breasts "furent garçonnés sur le blé." The *Dictionnaire du moyen français* (DMF)[13] would have us say that her breasts "were abused on the flour," but this is more aggressive than the scene allows and it loses the literal sense of *garçonnés* which describes the fumbling actions of a *garçon*. Perhaps the line could be translated to say her breasts "were manhandled on the flour", but the dactylic "manhandled," while keeping the personal sense of the action, is also a little too crude and, quite frankly, difficult to integrate into a verse line. We have therefore opted to elaborate on the metaphor suggested by the flour mill, and so our Miller flirts with The Second Lady by commenting on her breasts, saying that "being dusted with flour, they were kneaded." Such a transformation maintains the light tone of the original, but also evokes the loaves of bread served at the Miller's table.

In other instances, it has been impossible to maintain even the tone at the site of the original pun or allusion. We have attempted to make up for these difficulties, however, by inserting, at other places in the text, similar habits of writing when we could do so without substantially altering or diminishing the original meaning. So, for example, "Le Deuxième Gentilhomme," stuck in the chicken coop, tells his companion (whose wife is being seduced outside) that he must be quiet "Et dussions-nous ici pourrir" (Even if we have to rot in here). In this instance, we have changed the line so that The Second Gentleman tells his fellow that "We must sit and be quiet and bear these hen-pecks!" The new English line evokes traditional tropes of abusive wives while referring to the plight of the men, listening to their wives' debauchery while trapped among the chickens in the coop. Such insertions are rare, but they seek to replace the many allusions and puns which refer to the chickens or which equate sex with either an economy of exchange or a fine meal. While many such references are lost from the French, we hope the *sense* of the original is retained by replacing these references in other parts of the English text.

The English text, therefore, might be best thought of as a verse adaptation rather than a translation. It is hoped that some of the vigor, humor and, indeed, silliness of the original is captured in a way which a literal, academic prose translation simply could not do. For those wishing a greater sense of academic integrity, the French is always present for comparison.[14] For those who want the feel of the original in a more accessible format, the English verse, we hope, will offer a pleasant reading experience. We also hope that those performing early drama, but not able to mount productions in French, will take advantage of the opportunity to produce a farce which maintains the character of the original. Such efforts, we feel, can only expand the number of people working with the practical problems of performing the farce and, therefore, can only expand our collective understanding of the genre.

Synopsis

A. Meeting of the two Roosters

1) [1-49] Two gentlemen (M. de la Papillionnière and M. de la Hannetonnière) meet and exchange civilities before accusing each other of frequenting the Miller's wife (MilW). When the discussion grows tense, the First Gentleman (1G) begs for peace and they both agree not to pursue the debate further.

B. The Miller and his Wife: financial woes and redeeming scheme

2) [50-119] The MilW enters singing, but the Miller (Mil) is in no mood for merriment. He has no money to win their court case. The MilW suggests that the two gentlemen who own their mill lust after her and will lend them money in the hope that the Mil's case should keep him away long enough for them to seduce her. The Mil is impressed, but his Wife simply asks him to go back to sleep.

C. First visit of the gentlemen: attracting the punters

3) [120-211] The IG enters, voicing his desire for the MilW. He hails the Mil. The MilW greets him at the door. The IG asks for the money he is owed. She tells him off for visiting her in broad daylight. He says he is madly in love with her, and she answers that she is a faithful wife. He warns her that there will be trouble if she rejects him. She grants him the pleasure of her body if he should lend her husband money to attend his trial. The IG eagerly vouches for a hundred ducats. They wake the Mil who acts surprised when the IG lends him money. Once the money has exchanged hands, the IG and the MilW agree to meet at 5 o'clock. He tells her that he will bring a capon, a goose and wine. He leaves.

4) [212-221] The Mil congratulates his wife and shows his joy before he is ordered to quickly go back to his bed. The Second Gentleman (IIG) arrives at the door.

5) [222-307] The IIG voices his desire for the MilW. He hails the Mil. The MilW tells him to lower his voice to avoid waking her husband. The IIG flirts with her. She tells him about their financial woes and the IIG says he will lend them one hundred and twenty Philippus and a hundred "sous" if she concedes to his will. She refuses at first, arguing that he is a married man, but then accepts if he swears to defend her honor. They wake the Mil. His wife explains that she has secured the money. He acts surprised and accepts the money. The IIG and the MilW agree to meet between six and seven. He leaves.

6) [308-329] The Mil is amazed by the money and the subtlety of women. He then plans to secretly watch the would-be lovers and be ready to intervene. His wife claims that she would rather die than be dishonored, but he assures her that he has everything planned.

D. The gentlemen's return and the Trap

7) [330-369] The IG comes back, and hails the MilW who admits him. He offers her wine before they eat the food. The Mil watches from a distance. The IG is eager to get down to business but the MilW wants to wait until after dinner. The IG asks how far the Mil has gone now. Seven leagues, she says. The IG doubts it. The Mil mumbles a warning to himself. The IG drinks to his lady. The Mil announces to the audience that the deal is almost sealed.

8) [370-387] The IIG arrives and knocks on the door. The MilW stalls while the IG, believing the Mil has returned, panics because he is unarmed. The MilW suggests that he hide in the chicken coop.

9) [388-444] The IIG offers his wine bottle. She shows him the feast on the table. In an aside, the spying Mil laughs at the IG stuck in the chicken coop. From the chicken coop, the IG expresses his surprise at seeing the IIG with the MilW. The IIG drinks to the MilW. The IG complains to himself that they are feasting on his wine and food. The IIG is eager to get to business but the MilW is not in a hurry. The Mil warns the

audience that he is watching. The IIG tries to seduce the MilW, but she wants to wait until after dinner. The Mil has heard enough and rushes to the door. The IIG panics and is directed to the chicken coop. The IG welcomes him in.

E. The Revenge of the Mil: turning the table

10) [445-481] The MilW opens the door for her husband. The IIG complains that the food he brought will be eaten. The Mil asks what is for dinner. She lists the food. Both the IG and IIG realize that their food will be eaten. The Mil sends his Wife to fetch the IG's wife for dinner. The IG fumes while the IIG tries to shut him up. The Mil sings a song whilst feasting, and the IG asks if he is making fun of them.

11) [482-499] The MilW arrives at the house of the First Lady (IL) and invites her to the mill. She accepts.

12) [500-552] The IL greets the Mil who welcomes her. He invites her to sit with him. He starts fondling her. The IG is outraged and the IIG tries to keep him quiet. The Mil asks his wife to invite over the Second Lady (IIL) whilst still fondling the IL. The Mil drinks to the IL, and the IG vents his anger. The Mil asks the IL if she would allow him to kiss her but she refuses. The Mil persists and wins. The IG is irate but, being convinced to remain quiet, despairs of his wife. The Mil cuts to the chase and they both vanish behind the curtain. The two gentlemen admit that it is a done deal.

13) [553-562] The MilW arrives at the house of the IIL and invites her back to the mill. The IIL accepts.

14) [563-584] The IG describes the actions of the Mil and the IL as they reappear on stage. The Mil asks if she was hurt during sex, but she says she is fine. The IG curses and the IIG is cruelly ironic. The IIL enters and the Mil drinks to her. The MilW notices that the IL is ill-disposed. She says she feels weak, so the MilW takes her home.

15) [585-634] The Mil courts the IIL who is impressed by the food and drink. The Mil says he has wanted her for four months. He remembers the day they almost had sex but were interrupted. The IIG is offended, but the IG tells him to accept the situation. The Mil invites the IIL to eat and drink. She praises millers for their romantic speech. The IG appreciates the situation, whilst the IIG curses. The Mil plays the neglected lover seeking pity. The IG curses him from the chicken coop. The IIL is afraid of being revealed, but the Mil brushes her fear away, and she gives in.

16) [635-658] The IIG is beside himself and the IG tries to keep him quiet, citing his own experience. The IG warns him that his madness will alert the Mil. A brawl ensues that attracts the attention of the Mil.

F. The Coming Out of the Gentlemen

17) [659-714] The Mil bids goodbye to his new lover and moves to the chicken coop. The IIL leaves while the Mil and his wife speculate about what is in the coop. He asks his wife to bring him the spit from the fire because he hears noises. The gentlemen admit defeat and come out. The Mil asks who put them there, threatening them with the spit. The IG asks for mercy. The MilW claims that they wanted to prank the Mil. He disagrees and threatens them. The MilW comes to their rescue. The two gentlemen tell the Mil that he can keep the money they lent him as a gift. Before he

accepts the deal, the Mil demands to know why they were in his chicken coop. The wife tries to deflect the question but the Mil shuts her up. They say they were scared of him because they both wanted to enjoy his wife, but that he ended up enjoying theirs.

G. Form and reform

18) [715-732] The Mil and the two gentlemen formalize their grievance in a set poetic form called a *rondeau triolet*. The Mil addresses the audience and concludes with the moral: "When he deceives, it's deception he'll receive." The show ends with a participatory song.

Notes

1. To better understand the behaviour of literary critics in addressing the farce see Mario Longtin "La farce comme on l'a voulue. Le savant et l'attrait de la diégèse," *Le Savant dans les lettres*, ed. Valérie Cangemi, Alain Corbellari, Ursula Bähler (Rennes: PUR, 2014), pp. 247-59.

2. André de La Vigne, "La farce du Meunier de qui le diable emporte l'âme en enfer," *Recueil de farces (1450-1550)*, ed. André Tissier, vol. IV (Paris: Droz, 1989), pp. 167-243; and the anonymous farce of "Regnault qui se marie à la Vollée," *Le Recueil de Florence. 53 farces imprimées à Paris vers 1515*, ed. Jelle Koopmans (Paradigme: Orléans, 2011), pp. 125-36.

3. André Tissier calls the text "La farce des deux Gentilshommes et le meunier," *Recueil de farces (1450-1550)*, ed. André Tissier, vol. 1 (Geneva: Droz, 1986), pp. 305-94. The same collection also contains a play entitled "Le poulier" (vol. XI), with a cast of four actors, not to be mistaken with our play. For clarity's sake, we will refer to our play as *La farce du Poulier*.

4. The manuscript is Paris, BnF fr. 24341. *La farce du Poulier à 6 personnages* is text 27 of 74. Based on the watermarks, the manuscript can be dated between 1564-71. See Jonathan Beck, *Théâtre et propagande aux débuts de la Réforme* (Geneva: Droz, 1986), p. 51. Denis Hüe and Mario Longtin have discovered that the scribe of both BnF fr. 24341 and BnF fr. 19184 is Jehan Le Hucher, Admiral of Robec and a rich miller from Rouen. The manuscripts are witness to the vibrant cultural life of Rouen. BnF fr. 24341 and BnF fr. 19184 can be accessed online through the *Bibliothèque nationale de France* portal, Gallica.

5. An investigation into the difference between manuscript and print production may be very fruitful.

6. Jelle Koopmans has long advocated for such an approach and is preparing a new history of the farce. For a good example of a contextual study, read Katell Lavéant, *Un théâtre des frontières. La culture dramatique dans les provinces du Nord aux XVe et XVIe siècles* (Orléans: Paradigme, 2011).

7. One cannot but think of Marion from *Le jeu de Robin et Marion*. She prefers Robin to the knight, and rebukes his advances; see Adam de la Halle, *Le jeu de Robin et Marion*. Ed. and trans. Jean Dufournet (1989; repr., Flammarion: Paris, 1998).

8. The names are translated as Cockschafferette and Butterflyette respectively.

9. In Paris, BnF fr. 19184 Le Hucher apologizes for his poor spelling first to his readers, than later to God Himself, saying he never learnt how to spell: "*Messieurs qui lisés en ce livre / Excussés l'homme s'y vous plaist / Car jamais n'aprint a escripre / De l'orthograffe ne sçaict que c'est*" "My lords who are reading in this book / Forgive the man, if you please, / Because I never learnt to write / I don't know the first thing about spelling"; "*Mon Dieu, mon roy, je te suplye / Me pardonner aprés ma vie / Les faultes qui sont en ce livre / Tant d'ortograffe que d'escripre*" "My God, my King, I beg you / Forgive me in the afterlife / The errors that are found in this book / whether of spelling or of writing," BnF fr. 19184, fos. 11v and 359v.

10. It goes without saying that the presentation of a Renaissance text in modern French spelling should only be pursued when a proper critical edition of the text with the original spelling is readily available to the academic community.

11. For a recent discussion, see Chris Given-Wilson, *Chronicles: The Writing of History in Medieval England* (London and New York: Hambledon and London, 2004), pp. 143-7.

12. See, for example, Nicholas Watson, "Theories of Translation," *The Oxford History of Literary Translation in English: Vol I to 1550*, ed. Roger Ellis (Oxford: OUP, 2008), pp. 73-4.
13. The electronic version of the dictionary is accessible at (http://www.atilf.fr/dmf/). Accessed 16 July 2015.
14. For a more literal approach to the translation of farces, see the collection of prose adaptations in *The Farce of the Fart and Other Ribaldries: Twelves Medieval French Plays in Modern English*, ed. and trans. by Jodi Enders (Philadelphia: University of Pennsylvania Press, 2011). While adhering more closely to her source texts by translating into prose, Enders attempts to preserve "the farce's precious essence" (p. 34) through the use of colloquial American slang and pop culture references.

La farce du Poulier à six personnages
(in modern French spelling)

[132v] Farce nouvelle à six personnages; c'est assavoir : deux Gentilshommes, le Meunier, la Meunière et les deux Femmes des deux Gentilshommes (habillées en damoiselles).
Le Premier Gentilhomme commence, et est la *farce du Poulier*.

    Premier Gentilhomme
Honneur, Cousin.

    Deuxième Gentilhomme
    Honneur aussi !

    Premier Gentilhomme
De vous voir joyeux suis ici
Puisque santé en vous racine.[1]

    Deuxième Gentilhomme
4 Je suis sain et dru, Dieu merci,
Et n'ai sur moi ne ça ne ci
De déplaisir à ma saisine.[2]

    Premier Gentilhomme
Qui déplaisir d'autrui machine,
8 C'est bien de droit qu'il soit banni !

    Deuxième Gentilhomme
L'homme qui le mal imagine
Et en son cœur a la racine,
Doit être des autres puni !

    Premier Gentilhomme
12 Vous êtes toujours bien garni
De cela que vous devez dire.

    Deuxième Gentilhomme
Garni comme vous !

    Premier Gentilhomme
    Mais, beau Sire,
Est-il bien à notre meunière ?

    Deuxième Gentilhomme
[133r] Qu'en sais-je, moi ?

---

[1] *raciner*: to take root.
[2] *saisine*: in one's possession.

Premier Gentilhomme

16   Par quelle manière
Le pourrai-je donques savoir
Vu qu'en faites votre devoir,
Car bien souvent vous y hantez[3]
20 Entour elle et y fréquentez
Le soir, la nuit et le matin.
On connaît bien votre latin
Et le gibier de votre chasse.
24 Mais n'av'ous point de peur qu'on sache[4]
Toutes vos allées et venues ?
Un délit fait dessous les nues
Est su, entendre le devez !

Deuxième Gentilhomme

28 Vraiment, Cousin, vous ne savez
Comment vous vous ramentevoir ![5]
Un chacun vous y a pu voir,
On me l'a donné à entendre,
32 Et puis vous me venez reprendre,
Moi, qui ne suis en rien coupable !
Vous êtes en parler muable
Et bien digne d'être repris !
36 Gardez que n'y soyez surpris :
La vérité serait connue.

Premier Gentilhomme

Autant d'écus que toute nue
Vous l'avez tenue à votre aise !

Deuxième Gentilhomme

40 Autant d'écus qu'à la renverse
Vous l'avez sur son lit jetée.
Dea ! Votre personne jetée[6]
Y sera ! Donnez-vous-en garde !

Premier Gentilhomme

44 Qui aura bon droit, ci le garde !
N'en faisons ne noise ne bruit.
On connaît à l'arbre le fruit
Et le bon vin à la liqueur !
48 Adieu je vous dis, de bon cœur,
Un jour ferons chère plénière.

---

[3] *hanter*: to roam around.
[4] *n'av'ous*: contraction for *n'avez vous*.
[5] *ramentevoir*: to remember.
[6] *dea*: imprecation (mdFr.) *diable*, devil.

                Meunière *entre en chantant*
        O, va ! La Meunière ! O va ! O, va ! La Meunière...

[133v]   Meunier *commence*
        Toujours tu trouveras manière
52   De chanter sans prendre souci.
        Ma foi, si je faisais ainsi,
        Tout irait sans devant derrière !
        J'ai souci de faire et défaire,
56   J'ai souci d'aller et venir,
        Je ne me saurais soutenir !
        Que maudit soit la trumelière ![7]

        Meunière
        Dieu ! Qu'avez-vous ?

        Meunier
                Notre matière
60   Se perdra, j'en ai grosse peur,
        Car j'ai affaire à un trompeur,
        Un sous d'êtrë, un trompereau.[8]
        Plusit à Dieu que le bourreau[9]
64   L'eut pendu à mon appétit !
        Il n'y a ne grand ne petit
        Qui ne le connaisse à la cour.
        Quand il arrive là, on acccourt
68   Vers lui : procureurs, avocats,
        Et sergens, et esperlucats...[10]
        Et prend argent à toutes mains.

        Meunière
        Il faut que l'un de ces demains
72   Que vous et moi nous y allions
        Et que fermement nous parlions
        Aux juges et à l'assistance ;
        Et si votre partie me tance,[11]
76   Je lui saurai bien que répondre.
        Je le ferai par de moi fondre
        Dans la terre, fût-il régent ![12]

---

[7] *trumelière*: easy woman.
[8] *trompereau*: liar, operator. The word is derived from *trompeur* with an added pejorative connotation provided by the 'eau' suffix.
[9] *plusit*: imperfect subjunctive of *plaire* (to please). In mdFr.: *plût à Dieu*.
[10] *esperlucats*: cunning young men.
[11] *tancer*: to quarrel.
[12] *régent*: person in a position of power. The term regent might evoke the figure of the Duke of Bedford in the context of Rouen.

Meunier

On ne plaide point sans argent.
80 Le diable emporte le procès
Et me fera mettre en décès
Vingt ans devant mon âge dû.

Meunière

Il n'est pas dit que l'on se tue !
84 [134r] Vous voulez-vous pendre ou défaire ?
Notre Dame ! Laissez-moi faire,
J'aurai de l'argent promptement.

Meunier

De l'argent ?

Meunière

Voire, finement !
88 Il n'est finesse qu'on ne fasse.

Meunier

Et, belle Dame, que je sache
Comme argent pourriez attraper ![13]
Je serais tant aise de voir
92 De l'argent pour à mon cas pourvoir
Des écus vingt, trente ou quarante...

Meunière

Nous en aurons plus de cinquante
Aussi rouges que séraphins,[14]
96 Mais il faudrait que fussions fins
Et que ne disions mot de rien.

Meunier

Par la Mort [bieu], je ferai bien
Le fin pour argent attraper.[15]
100 En [v]ois-tu aucuns à piper[16]
A ton entente ou jobelin ?[17]

---

[13] *comme*: (mdFr.) *comment*.
[14] *Aussi rouges que séraphins*: of the purest gold (Tissier, v. 95, p. 339).
[15] *Argent pour le fin attraper*. We have modified the word order, and adopted Tissier's suggestion (v. 99, p. 340).
[16] *piper*: to catch, to fool.
[17] *jobelin*: deceptive discourse.

Meunière

Les Maîtres de notre moulin
Sont fort amoureux de mon corps.
104 Si vous feigniez aller dehors
Environ vingt jours ou un mois
Nous aurions des écus de poids
En leur faisant la ruse accroire,
108 Et puis revenez sur votre erre,
Quand de l'argent serez muni.
Jamais un renard pris au nid
Ne fut si peneux qu'ils seront.[18]
112 Possible qu'ils nous donneront
De notre moulin les louages
Avecque tous les arriérages
Qu'on leur devait du temps passé.[19]

Meunier

116 Par la mort bieu, c'est bien pensé !
[134v] Que dois-je faire pour complaire ?

Meunière

Dormez-vous et me laissez faire,
Je suis de langage pourvu !

Premier Gentilhomme

120 N'aurai-je point une venue
De la femme de mon meunier ?[20]
A peu près de regnïer suis
La loi Nouvelle et l'Ancïenne !
124 Sang bieu, si tenir la puis mienne
A mon désir et mon entente
Je la baiserai des fois trente,
En faisant l'amoureux délit !
128 Oh ! Que la tenir sur un lit
Pour la ribauder quinze jours…[21]
Vers elle m'en vais tout le cours
Afin que mon ennui soit hors.
Ho ! Meunier !

Meunier

132   Dites que je dors
Hardiment, il ne s'en faut guère.

---

[18] *peneux*: disappointed, sheepish.
[19] *qu'on leur devait*: modified from the original phrase: *qu'on leur debvons*.
[20] We removed 8 lines the scribe transcribed by mistake. He later transcribes them at their proper location (lines 332-9). *De moy n'eust pas eu un denyer / Ce n'eust esté de par sa femme / Car son coeur le myen tant enflame / Que j'en suys presque au mourir / Vouecy l'heure que secourir / Elle m'a dict qu'elle me poura bien / Je m'y envoys sans craindre rien / De tant atendre je ne puys.*
[21] *ribauder*: to debauch.

MEUNIÈRE
Honneur ! Monsieur.

PREMIER GENTILHOMME
Dieu gard, Meunière !
Aurai-je de l'argent de vous ?

MEUNIER
136 L'argent est bien court endroit nous:[22]
"Qui cherche argent, cherche débat !"

MEUNIÈRE
Comment avez-vous pris l'ébat
De venir à cette heure ici ?

[135r] PREMIER GENTILHOMME
140 Oui, car (je) suis à demi transi !
Si de vous ne suis secouru…
A peu que n'en ai encouru
La mort, par le Dieu de Nature.

MEUNIÈRE
144 Ce me serait une laidure[23]
Et une honte diffamable
Que d'être trouvée varïable
Au déshonneur de mon mari.

PREMIER GENTILHOMME
148 Vous me faites le cœur marri
Et me rendez du tout confus.
Si vous faites de moi refus,
Dites-le-moi, je m'en irai !
152 Mais par la Mort, je vous ferai
Du déplaisir et de l'ennui !

MEUNIÈRE
Ce ne saurait être aujourd'hui
Si vous ne parlez à Lucas
156 Et le conseiller de son cas
Honnêtement en lieu secret.
On nous veut passer par décret
Notre héritage à nous sujet.
160 Pour venir à la fin du jet,
Prêter nous faut argent à force,
Et puis après que l'on s'efforce
Faire de moi ce qu'on pourra !

---

22 *endroit nous*: around us, in our house.
23 *laidure*: insult.

Premier Gentilhomme

164 Ah ! Pensez qu'il ne demeurera
Pas envers moi pour cent ducats !
Debout Meunier !

Meunière

Debout Lucas !
Dormirez-vous toute ajournée ?

Premier Gentilhomme

168 Or ça, Meunier ! Une fournée
D'argent, je vous ferai quittance.[24]

Meunier

Toujours survient quelqu'un qui tance
Et se monstre mon ennemi.

Meunière

172 [135v] Il est encor tout endormi[25]
Et a fait un terrible somme.
Votre Monsieur le Gentilhomme
Qui vient avec nous deviser.
176 Il s'est bien voulu amuser,
Dont je mercie son personnage !
Nous parlions de notre héritage
Qu'on dit qu'il nous sera tolie,[26]
180 Et il dit que vous ferez folie
Si vous n'y êtes vertüeux,
Car pour un cent écus ou deux
Vous jouïrez paisiblement.

Meunier

184 Cent écus! C'est bien largement!
Il suffirait de quatre-vingts
Pour payer fausses lettres, vins,
Arriérages, mises et dettes.
188 Par ma foi, de toutes recettes
Je ne sache qu'un gros qui court ![27]

Premier Gentilhomme

Dea, Meunier, pour le faire court,
Pour un cent écus d'or de poids,
Je vous les prête.

---

[24] *quittance*: a written attestation of a loan.
[25] *encor*: poetic license for *encore*.
[26] *tolir*: to take away.
[27] *gros*: coin of little value.

Meunier
192   Je vous en dois !

Premier Gentilhomme
C'est tout un, vous paierez toujours !
Mais ne faites pas longs séjours,
Partez-moi plus tôt que plus tard.
196 Je les avais boutés à part
Pour cuider un paiement parfaire.
Allez, pensez à votre affaire…
Et pensez tôt de revenir !

Meunier
200 Cent écus! C'est pour survenir
De tout mon affaire à honneur.

Premier Gentilhomme
Adieu, Meunier.

Meunier
               Adieu, Monsieur.

Premier Gentilhomme
Adieu, Meunière.

Meunière
               Monsieur, adieu !

Premier Gentilhomme
204 Dites de revenir au lieu
[136r] Que je sois de l'heure averti.

Meunière
Mais que le meunier soit parti…
A cinq heures ?

Premier Gentilhomme
               Voilà le cas !
208 J'apporterai, pour le repas,
Un gras chapon avec une oie.

Meunière
Et du vin.

Premier Gentilhomme
             Pour faire la joie,
Puis nos plaisirs seront vaincus !

Meunier

212 Ça, de par Dieu, j'ai cent écus !
Cent écus d'or ! Mort bieu, je t'aime !
Tu es de finesse la crème
Et subtille par-dessus tous.

Meunière

216 Ce n'est encor rien, taisez-vous.
Dormez-vous, faites bonne mine,
Je suis pour Messieurs assez fine…
Mot, voici l'autre qui revient !
220 Vous orrez de moi le maintient,
Mais ne sonnez mot quoiqu'il soit.

Deuxième Gentilhomme

L'amour d'une femme déçoit
Le cœur de l'homme assez souvent.
224 Ci faut-il plus tôt que le vent
Que je trouve façon d'aller
A la Meunière ou au Meunier
Qui tient mon cœur à sa saisine.
228 Ce m'est force que je domine
D'elle, ou mourir me convient,
Car cent mille fois me souvient
De sa convenance courtoise.
Ho ! Meunier.

Meunière

232   Faites basse noise,[28]
Monsieur, votre meunier repose.

Deuxième Gentilhomme

Ah ! Mon tétin, m'amour, ma rose ![29]
Te tinssé-je à ma volonté ?[30]
236 Tant j'ai le cœur entalenté[31]
[136v] D'accomplir ce que je veux dire !
Où est le meunier ?

Meunière

          Il dort, Sire.
Il est un peu mal disposé.

Deuxième Gentilhomme

Qu'est-ce qu'il a ?

---

[28] *faites basse noise*: be quiet.
[29] *m'amour*: (mdFr.) *mon amour*.
[30] *tinssé-je*: 1st pers. sing. subjunctive imperfect of the verb *tenir* (to hold).
[31] *entalenté*: eager.

Meunière

240 Il n'a osé,
Le temps passé rien emprunter,
Et c'est bien laissé endetter
Notre héritage de village
244 De cent francs tout en arriérage
Et est de le conter honteux.
Si nous trouvions de bons prêteurs[32]
Ou gens baillant argent à rente,
248 Ma foi, toute à l'heure présente
Notre héritage irait recouvrer.
Vous le verriez, par Dieu, trotter
Comme un savetier portant cuir!

Deuxième Gentilhomme

252 S'il vous plaît me laisser jouïr
De votre corps un jour, sans plus,
Je prêterai six-vingts Ph'lippus[33]
Avecques cent sous de monnaie.

Meunière

256 Hélas, Monsieur je n'oserais.
Comment, vous êtes marïé !

Deuxième Gentilhomme

L'amour de vous m'a charrïé
Et fait en cestui lieu venir.[34]
260 S'il vous plaît me laisser jouïr
A mon grand désir et entente,
Vous aurez à l'heure présente
Six-vingts Ph'lippus d'or et de poids
264 Avecques un cent sous tournois
De monnaië que vous aurez.

Meunière

Au moins, Monsieur, considérez
De garder l'honneur qui s'ensuit…

Deuxième Gentilhomme

268 Mot ! Je n'y viendrai que de nuit
Et ci ferons chère papale.

La Meunière

Je l'accepte.

---

[32] *prêteurs* : pronounced *prêteux* for the rhyme.
[33] *ph'lippus*: most probably the currency developed by Philip the Good. The word was abbreviated on the coin which explains the pronounciation.
[34] *en cestui lieu*: (mdFr.) *en ce lieu-ci*.

[137r]   Deuxième Gentilhomme
           Ça, que je parle
Au meunier pour bailler argent.³⁵

           La Meunière
272 Pas ne sera ci négligent
    S'il ne pense de son profit.

           Deuxième Gentilhomme
    Debout, Meunier !

           Meunière
                       Il est confit
    Cette journée-ci à dormir.

           Meunier
276 Tu me fais tout le sang frémir !
    Comme cette-ci me tempête !

           Meunière
    Vous ne pouvez lever la tête ?
    Tant dormir, ce n'est pas santé !
280 Voici Monsieur qui s'est vanté
    Et dit pour nous faire plaisir
    De nous prêter d'un bon désir
    Six-vingts Ph'lippus, avec cent sous,
284 Afin que nous soyons résous³⁶
    De l'héritage à notre vie.

           Meunier
    Saint Jean ! Dieu lui doint bonne vie³⁷
    Et le tienne en prospérité !

           Deuxième Gentilhomme
288 Tenez, les voilà tout comptés !
    Pensez tôt de votre profit.
    Estimez que mon cœur ne fit,
    Comme pouvez apercevoir,
292 Jamais de meilleur vouloir.
    Ne prêtai argent [de] ma vie³⁸
    Qu'à vous deux, je vous certifie.
    Quand partez-vous, que je le sache ?

           Meunière
296 Monsieur, je le tiendrais pour lâche
    S'il ne partait expressément.

---

35   *bailler*: (mdFr.) *donner*, to give
36   *résous*: (mdFr.) *résolus*, to be done with.
37   *doint*: (mdFr.) *donne*, give.
38   *à ma vie*. We have modified the preposition

MEUNIER

Je partirai présentement
Devant qu'il soit heure et demie.

DEUXIÈME GENTILHOMME

300 Dites de revenir ma mie.
Quand pourrai-je de soir venir ?

MEUNIÈRE

Je pourrai à vous survenir
Entre six et sept. C'est bonne heure ?

DEUXIÈME GENTILHOMME

304 [137v] Je n'ai pas peur que je ne meurs
D'attendre si tant ! Or adieu !
Preparez la place et le lieu,
De revenir j'aurai le soin.

MEUNIER

308 Ça ! Ça ! J'ai de l'or à plein poing !
Femmes sont fines à merveilles :
Quand l'homme fait grandes oreilles[39]
Il ne lui en peut que bien prendre !
312 A mon fait, il me faut entendre.
Tout *primo*, il me faut aller
Et les laisser un peu parler
Ensemble et eux deviser.
316 *Secondo*, il me faut aviser
Que de droit le guet je ferai.
Le celui que j'attraperai
Avec ma femme nu à nu,
320 Premier qu'il soit de moi connu,
Je lui montrerai mon effort !

MEUNIÈRE

J'aimerais mieux être à la mort
Que fisse de mon corps offense.
324 Mais ayez en vous la scïence
De survenir bref après eux.
Ce que je fais, c'est pour le mieux.
Ainsi vous le devez entendre.

MEUNIER

328 Laisse-moi ce fait entreprendre.
Tout viendra bien, j'y ai pensé.

---

[39] *faire grandes oreilles*: to act like a fool (referring to the fool's bonnet). *Grandes oreilles* (literally 'big ears') are also associated with donkeys, and their proverbial stupidity. We prefer this interpretation because of the words *folie* and *fol* found in the conclusion of the farce. Tissier offers the gloss: listening with docility.

Premier Gentilhomme

Serai-je point récompensé
Des cent écus de mon meunier ?
332 De moi n'eut pas eu un denier
Si n'eut été de par sa femme,
Car son cœur le mien tant enflamme
Que j'en suis presquë au mourir
336 Voici l'heure que secourir
El(le) m'a dit qu'elle pourra bien
Je m'y en vais sans craindre rien
De tant endurer je ne puis !
Holà, ho !

Meunière

340   Qui est-cë à l'huis ?

Premier Gentilhomme

[138r] Vous ai-je failli de promesse ?

Meunière

Réverence à votre noblesse !
Vous êtes venu sans servant ?

Premier Gentilhomme

344 Je n'y veux aucun poursuivant[40]
Car le troisième point n'y faut.
Goûtons un peu que ce vin vaut,
Puis nous ferons collatïon.

Meunier

348 Si vous faites cul-tatïon,[41]
Meunière, avec Monsieur le Brave,
Par la Mort bieu, si je n'enclave[42]
Ma dague dedans votre sein !

Premier Gentilhomme

352 Mon cœur n'a garde d'être sain,
Meunière, quand je vous contemple,
[Jusqu'à] ce que votre cœur emple[43]
Et assouvisse mon vouloir.

Meunière

356 Puisque de moi avez pouvoir,
Après souper nous ébattrons.

---

[40] *poursuivant*: a junior herald of arms. Here *poursuivant* has a sexual connotation linking actions in arms and sexual prowess.
[41] *cultation*: playful neologism found only in our text, which refers to a sexual 'somersault'.
[42] *enclaver ma dague*: to plunge my dagger.
[43] *jusque ce que. Empler*: to fulfil.

Premier Gentilhomme
Où peut être notre patron
Depuis l'heure que parti est ?

Meunière
Bien à sept lieux !

Premier Gentilhomme
360   Par Dieu, non est !

Meunière
Il ne s'en saurait falloir guère !

Meunier
Monsieur de La Papillonnière
Voudrait que je fusse nïais ![44]
364 S'il n'est de par moi relïé
Aujourd'hui, que l'on me dessire.[45]

Premier Gentilhomme
Je bois à vous.

Meunière
        Grand merci, Sire !

Meunier
Voilà tantôt le marché fait
368 Et tant de tels galants on sait
Qui n'en tiennent compte ne taille.[46]

Deuxième Gentilhomme
Voici l'heure qu'il faut que j'aille[47]
[138v] Voir celle-là qui m'a promis
372 Que serai l'un de ses amis
C'est bien de droit que j'y compare.[48]
Je pense, moi, qu'elle prépare
Son logis pour me recevoir.
376 Mon sang ne se fait qu'émouvoir
De dépit que déjà n'y suis.
Ouvrez ! Ouvrez !

Meunière
        Qui est-ce à l'huis ?

---

[44] *niais* (simple, stupid) and *relié* (tied down) are meant to rhyme, they are spelled *nyé* / *relyé* in the manuscript.

[45] *dessire:* tear to pieces.

[46] *ne tenir compte ne taille*: to give without restriction.

[47] Folio 138v starts with a line mistakenly repeated from folio 138r (*Apres souper nous esbaton*) and then crossed out.

[48] *Comparer* (alternative spelling: *comparoir*): to attend, to show up. In this specific context, the word is polysemic and suggests the effort needed to acquire something: lots of money or sexual energy.

Premier Gentilhomme

Sang bieu, j'ai entendu quelqu'un !
380 Encor j'ai laissé mon verdun[49]
Et ma dague pour me défendre.

Deuxième Gentilhomme

Holà ! Holà !

Meunière

Il faut entendre.

Premier Gentilhomme

Mon Dieu que j'ai le cœur marri !
384 Je crois que c'est votre mari.
Jésus, il m'ira publier !

Meunière

Cachez-vous dedans ce poulier
Jusqu'à ce qu'il soit retourné.

Deuxième Gentilhomme

388 Je n'ai pas longtemps séjourné
Après l'heure délimitée.
Que cette bouteille boutée[50]
Me soit en un lieu proprement ;
392 Voilà pour faire gentiment
Le banquet pour l'amour de vous.

Meunière

Semblablement, voici pour nous
Banquet que j'ai tôt apprêté.
396 Est-il rien de novalité,[51]
Monsieur de La Hannetonière ?

Meunier

Monsieur de La Papillonnière
Est prochain voisin de nos poules.
400 Et pensez qu'il n'a pas les couilles
En si bon point comme il avait.

---

[49] *verdun*: a long and narrow sword made in Verdun, France.
[50] *boutée*: given.
[51] *novalité*: (mdFr.) *nouveauté*, novelty, news.

Premier Gentilhomme

 Et qui, tous les diables, savait
 Que Monsieur de La Hannetonière
404 [139r] Vint visiter notre meunière
 Comme moi ? Ah, je suis surpris !
 Une autre fois serai appris[52]
 De faire mon cas plus asseur ![53]

Deuxième Gentilhomme

408 Sav'ous que vous ferez, ma sœur ?[54]
 Je bois à vous à verre plein.

Premier Gentilhomme

 Par le saint Sang bieu ! Le vilain
 Boit mon vin et mange mon pain !
412 Encor n'en oserais parler.
 Si je me mets à dévaler,[55]
 Le jeu ne te sera pas beau !

Deuxième Gentilhomme

 Allons derrière le rideau[56]
416 Accomplir le jeu d'amourettes.[57]

La Meunière

 Non, pas encor…

Meunier

    Eh ! Je vous guette,
 Monsieur Le Hannetoneur,
 Vous ne venez pas par honneur
420 A ma maison, c'est chose seure ![58]

Deuxième Gentilhomme

 Me secour'rez-vous à cette heure ?
 Serai-je de ma douleur hors ?

Meunière

 Après souper, prenez le corps
424 Faites-en à votre plaisir.
 Mais devisons tout à loisir,
 Mon cœur s'embrase en vous voyant…

---

[52] *être appris*: to be warned.
[53] *asseur* (verb *assurer*): to make more certain.
[54] *sav'ous*: contraction for *savez-vous*.
[55] *dévaler* : to rush down.
[56] *le rideau*: an indirect stage direction on the presence of a curtain; most probably referring to the backstage curtain.
[57] *jeu d'amourettes*: sexual activities.
[58] *seure*: (mdFr.) *sure*, certain. Spelling with unresolved diphthong to accommodate the rhyme with *heure*.

Meunier

    Ah ! Je n'en puis endurer tant
428 J'en perds sens, mémoire et la voix !
    Par la Mort bieu, je m'y en vois,[59]
    En ce lieu, je ne puis plus vivre ;
    Il faut contrefaire de l'ivre…
432 Sang bieu, ilz seront égorgés !
    Ouvrez ! Ouvrez !

Meunière

                Ne vous bougez !
    Qui vous fait ainsi tournoyer ?

Deuxième Gentilhomme

    J'ai entendu notre meunier.
436 [139v] Jésus Christ, je suis diffamé !

Meunière

    Oh ! Jésus !

Deuxième Gentilhomme

            Je l'ai réclamé.
    Qu'Il me préserve en cette place !

Meunière

    Lancez-vous tôt en cette place,
440 Haut, au poulier, à nos gélines,[60]
    Car ses pensées sont si tant fines
    Qu'il vous tuerait, c'est chose seure.[61]

Premier Gentilhomme

    Vous y voilà pris à cette heure,
444 A ce poulier, ainsi que moi !

Meunier

    Je sais bien, moi, que je mettrai
    L'huis hors des gons si tu ne m'ouvres!

Meunière

    Mon Dieu, voici une belle œuvre,
448 Jamais je ne vis votre pair ![62]

Meunier

    Par la Mort bieu, je veux pomper ![63]

---

59   *je m'y en vois*: (mdFr.) *j'y vais* or *je m'en vais*.
60   *gélines*: hens.
61   See note on line 420: *seure* / *heure*.
62   Here *pair* (mdFr.: *paire*), rhymes with *pomper*. This means that the « er » is not pronounced « é » as in modern French « aimer » but like « amer » (bitter).
63   *pomper*: to feast.

####### Deuxième Gentilhomme
A Dieu command notre souper !
Il sera tantôt dévoré.

####### Meunier
452 Or ça, mon petit con doré,
Qu'as-tu accoutré[64] à repaître ?

####### Meunière
Chômez-vous. Vous devez connaître[65]
Qu'on avons assez et de bon.[66]
456 Voilà du bouilli, du jambon,
Pain, vin, perdrïaux et mauvis...

####### Premier Gentilhomme
C'est fait ! Nous voilà déservis !
A tous les diables, le soulard !

####### Meunier
460 Que ce vin ici est gaillard
Et un souper pris d'un bon zèle !
Va moi quérir ma damoiselle,
Dame de La Papillonnière.
464 Qu'el(le) vienne avec moi faire chère
Et qu'el(le) ne se soucie de rien.

[140r] ####### Meunière
Je m'y en vais.

####### Meunier
                  Mais sais-tu bien ?
Ne me cesse pas de courir.

####### Premier Gentilhomme
468 Ce vilain me fera mourir.
C'est ma femme qu'il envoie querre.
Si jamais il est bruit de guerre,
Je le ferai bien régenter !

####### Deuxième Gentilhomme
472 S'il nous ot ci parlementer
Il abaissera notre ton.

---

[64] *accoutrer*: to prepare (here relating to food).
[65] *Chômez-vous*: rest.
[66] *Qu'on avons* : cf. *que nous avons*. 3rd pers. sing. pronoun followed by a 1st pers. plur. ending is characteristic of Norman French dialect.

MEUNIER, *en chantant*
Ho ! Biboton, biboton, biboton !⁶⁷
Encore, encore, encore, encore !
476 Ho ! Biboton, biboton, biboton !
Encore un horion !⁶⁸

PREMIER GENTILHOMME
Mais pense-t-il qu'on en riions ?⁶⁹
Il a beau chanter, ci je dance !⁷⁰
480 Je n'ai point de réjouissance.
Que maudit de Dieu soit ton ventre !

MEUNIÈRE
Il ne vous déplaît pas si j'entre
Et que je fasse à l'arrivée,⁷¹
484 Ma damoiselle la privée ?⁷²
Lucas à vous se recommande
Et vous prie, d'une amour grande,
Que vous en venez quant et moi.

PREMIÈRE DAMOISELLE
Et où, Meunière ?

MEUNIÈRE
488   Avecques moi,
Plaisanter et mener lïesse.

PREMIERE DAMOISELLE
Je n'oserais.

MEUNIÈRE
                   Et pourquoi est-ce ?
Ah! Il n'y a point de danger
492 Il vous fera bien étranger⁷³
Mélancolie, si vous l'avez.

PREMIERE DAMOISELLE
Allons doncques, mais vous savez
Que longtemps je ne puis pas mettre.
496 Si Monsieur mon mari, mon Maître,
[140v] Survenait, je serais tancée.⁷⁴

---

67 *bibotons*: to drink. Neologism made from the Latin *bibere*.
68 *horion*: a blow.
69 *qu'on en riions*: (mdFr.) *que nous en riions* or *qu'on en rie*.
70 *ci* for *ici*: here.
71 *faire à l'arrivée* : without ceremony or fuss.
72 *privée*: friend.
73 *étranger*: to forget, to leave behind.
74 *être tancée*: to be punished.

####### Meunière

Je ne suis pas si insensée
De vous laisser faire séjour.

####### Première Damoiselle

Bonsoir, Meunier.

####### Meunier

500   Bonjour, bonjour !
Bienvenue, ma damoiselle.

####### Meunière

Asseyez-vous sur cette selle[75]
Afin que soyez à votre aise.

####### Première Damoiselle

Grand merci.

####### Meunière

504   Ne vous déplaise.

####### Première Damoiselle

Laissez Meunier…

####### Premier Gentilhomme

                 Quoi ? Il la baise !
Méchant qu'est-ce que tu feras ?

####### Deuxième Gentilhomme

Par la Mort bieu, tu te tairas
508   Et dussions-nous ici pourrir !

####### Meunier

Viens ça, va moi encor quérir
Madame La Hannetonière.
Qu'el(le) vienne avec moi faire chère
512   Que je la traite à mon vouloir.

####### Première Damoiselle

Eh ! Vous faites plus que devoir,
C'est trop de coût pour cette fois!

####### Meunier

Ma damoiselle, à vous je bois.

####### Première Damoiselle

516   Ah ! Meunier, la vôtre merci !

---

[75] *Seez-vous sur cette selle.* The mdFr. *asseyez* offers one more syllable in order to complete the octosyllabic line.

Premier Gentilhomme

De glaive tu aies le cœur transi
Tant tu nous fais ci chagriner.

Meunier

Sav'ous que viens d'adeviner[76]
520 Ma damoiselle à cette fois ?

Première Damoiselle

Et quoi Meunier ?

Meunier

        Par sainte Croix,
Je vous voudrais bien demander
Si je vous voulais embrasser
524 [141r] Si vous me laisseriez point faire ?

Premiere Damoiselle

Déportez-vous de cette affaire,[77]
Car nous n'oserions en ce lieu.

Meunier

Et pourquoi ?

Première Damoiselle

        C'est « offense Dieu » !

Meunier

528 « Offense Dieu » ? Ah, ce n'est rien,
D'autres que nous l'offensent bien !
Laissez-moi goûter de l'amorce.

Premier Gentilhomme

Elle fera ta male bosse :
532 Traître, méchant, méseau rendu ![78]

Deuxième Gentilhomme

Tant de fois, je t'ai défendu,
Mort bieu, que tu ne die un mot !
Si cet ivrogne ici nous ot,
536 Qui est maintenant à son aise,
Il nous pourrait bien, par saint Blaise,[79]
Faire mourir de mort infâme.

---

[76] *sav'ous*: contraction of *savez-vous*; *adeviner*: to imagine.
[77] *déporter*: to break away, to desist.
[78] *méseau* (other form: *mésel*): leper. In the context, according to the editor Tissier (p. 375 v. 532), the insult *méseau rendu* would refer to a monk suffering from leprosy.
[79] *saint Blaise*: invoked against throat illnesses. Here, one Gentleman is trying to silence the other.

PREMIER GENTILHOMME
Quoi, il veut le faire à ma femme !

DEUXIÈME GENTILHOMME
540 Et bien, combien as-tu perdu ?

PREMIER GENTILHOMME
J'aimerais mieux qu'il fut pendu,
J'avoue Dieu et Marie la belle !

MEUNIER
Le ferons-nous, ma damoiselle,
544 A celle fin que sois guéri ?

PREMIÈRE DAMOISELLE
N'en parlez pas à mon mari.

MEUNIER
J'aimerais mieux être damné.
Allons faire le démené[80]
548 Que j'embatte votrë écu.[81]

PREMIER GENTILHOMME
Ah, c'est fait, me voilà cocu !
Quel(le) douleur pour pauvres maris !

DEUXIÈME GENTILHOMME
Pour un, il en fait deux marris.

PREMIER GENTILHOMME
552 Ce fait mon que tuer le vois ![82]

MEUNIÈRE
Je m'étais boutée à la voie
De vous venir voir, damoiselle.
[141v] Mon mari a la pensée telle
556 Qu'il vous veut à souper donner.

DEUXIÈME DAMOISELLE
Je ne le serais guerdonner[83]
Du grand service qu'il me fait.

MEUNIÈRE
Voilà qu'il m'a dit en effet
560 Que vous en venez quant et moi.[84]

---

[80] *faire le démené*: to have sex.
[81] *embattre l'écu*: to attack the shield. In a sexual context: to penetrate a woman, to have sexual intercourse.
[82] *Ce fait mon*: certainly, undoubtedly.
[83] *guerdonner*: to repay.
[84] *quant et moi*: with me.

Deuxième Damoiselle

Vraiment, très volontiers j'irai,
Mais il sera récompensé.

Premier Gentilhomme

Qui, tous les diables, eut pensé
564 Que ma femme eut fait cet accord
Qu'à ce méchant vilain et ord[85]
Eut abandonné son maujoint ?[86]
Le vilain, je l'os, là, où il geint !
568 Le pourceau, il me fait Jenin ![87]

Meunier

Vous ai-je blessée ?

Première Damoiselle

Nenin, nenin !

Premier Gentilhomme

Tu blesseras ta male rage !

Deuxième Gentilhomme

Savoure un petit ce breuvage
572 Et prends patïence en ton cœur.

Première Damoiselle

Au moins, gardez-moi mon honneur,
Mon ami, je me fie à vous.

Deuxième Damoiselle

Bonsoir, Meunier.

Meunier

Ci fa[is-je] vous ![88]
576 Vous soyez la très bienvenue !
Ça ! Ça ! Il faut faire revue
Sur notre vin. Je bois à vous !

Meunière

Ma damoiselle, qu'avez-vous ?
580 Vous me semblez en déplaisance.[89]

---

[85] *ord*: dirty, repulsive.
[86] *maujoint*: the sex of a woman.
[87] *faire Jenin*: to cuckold.
[88] *Sy fasy vous. Ci fa[is-je] vous*: I salute you in return.
[89] *déplaisance*: general unhappiness.

Première Damoiselle
Las, il m'est pris une faillance[90]
En ce lieu, je me sens malsaine.[91]

Meunier
Il vaut mieux que tu la ramènes.

Meunière
[142r] Je le veux bien.

Première Damoiselle
584   Allons Meunière.

Meunier
Ça, Madame La Hannetonière,
J'ai de vous voir réjouïssance.

Deuxième Damoiselle
Je suis venue en bonne chance :
588 Voici pain, vin, vïande assez !

Meunier
Il y a quatre mois passés
Que j'ai de vous traiter envie.

Deuxième Damoiselle
Je vous remercie.

Meunier
                Fûtes-vous mie
592 Cinq jours dedans notre moulin ?
Vos tétins aussi blancs que lin
Furent garçonnés sur le blé…[92]

Deuxième Damoiselle
Mon corps fut par vous accolé,
596 Mais je ne vous laissai pas faire.

Meunier
Sang bieu, il ne s'en fallut guère
Que je ne mise au pertuis ![93]
Sans une de derrière l'huis,
600 J'allais mêler mes deux genoux.

Deuxième Gentilhomme
Sang bieu ! Il se moque de nous.
Il livre babil à la mienne !

---

[90] *faillance*: moment of weakness.
[91] *malsaine*: sick, unhealthy.
[92] *garçonnés*: handled roughly, manhandled.
[93] *mettre au pertuis*: sexual penetration.

Premier Gentilhomme

      Et penses-tu donc qu'il se tienne
604   Qu'il ne lui fasse comme à l'autre ?
      Que mon corps soit bouilli en peautre[94]
      S'il lui faut ! Ah, je le vois bien !

Meunier

      Ma damoiselle, n'épargnez rien :
608   Buvez, mangez de cœur joyeux !

Deuxième Damoiselle

      Ces meuniers sont tant amoureux !
      Il n'est finesse qui n'en sorte.

Deuxième Gentilhomme

      Et tais-toi ! Tais-toi, pauvre sotte !
612   Tiens-tu babil à ce badaud ?

Meunier

      Si j'avais vu votre bidaut[95]
      Je serais guéri, ce me semble.
      [142v] Mais pour voir un peu s'il ressemble
616   A celui de ma ménagère.

Premier Gentilhomme

      Mais regardez comme il s'ingère
      A parler qui le veut ouïr
      Pour mieux de la femme jouïr.

Deuxième Gentilhomme

620   C'est un méchant, pour tout potage !
      J'ai tel dépit et telle rage
      Que je ne sais à qui le dire.

Meunier

      Dame, vous plaît-il m'éconduire ?
624   Serai-je remis en vigueur ?

Premier Gentilhomme

      Mais ta male roide langueur !
      Tu l'as bien fait à nos dépends !

Meunier

      Me tiendrez-vous ainsi suspends[96]
628   En misère et calamité ?

---

[94] *peautre*: an alloy of lead and tin (also called pewter). It is worth noting that usurers and money lenders are ususally tortured in Hell in boiling metal.
[95] *bidaut*: the sex of a woman.
[96] *suspends*: (mdFr.) *en suspend*, waiting.

Deuxième Damoiselle
Et voire... mais, si récité
Etait à mon mari, où qu'il soit,
Et qu'un jour il s'en aperçoit,
632 Toujours me le reprochera.

Meunier
Le diable emport(e) qui lui dira !

Deuxième Damoiselle
Allons donc, je m'y accorde.

Deuxième Gentilhomme
Notre Dame, miséricorde !
636 Il tient ma femme, ce méchant !

Premier Gentilhomme
Par Dieu, vous quitterez ce chant
Ou j'étranglerai votre gorge !
Il a fait une heure d'horloge
640 A la mienne et tu m'as fait taire !

Deuxième Gentilhomme
Eh, il la tient !

Premier Gentilhomme
    Qu'y veux-tu faire ?
Tu sais qu'il a le diable au corps !

Deuxième Gentilhomme
Ah ! Mes amis miséricord(e)s !
644 Il souffle et pète tout d'un train
Et faut-il que je sois contraint
De l'ouïr ainsi remuer !

Premier Gentilhomme
[143r] Vous nous voulez faire tuer ?
648 A cette heure, vous vous tairez !

Deuxième Gentilhomme
Par la Mort bieu, vous mentirez !

Premier Gentilhomme
Ci ferez-vous, par la vertu !
Et comment, je me suis bien tu.

Deuxième Gentilhomme
Au meurtre !

Premier Gentilhomme
    A l'aide !

Deuxième Gentilhomme
652   Que ferai-je ?

Premier Gentilhomme
Tu te tairas.

Deuxième Gentilhomme
              Plutôt mourrai-je !
A l'aide ! Messieurs, je suis mort !

Premier Gentilhomme
Pourquoi diable cries-tu si fort ?

Deuxième Gentilhomme
656   Tu m'as affolé par les couilles !

Meunier
Il y a quelqu'un à nos poules !
Par la Mort bieu, je m'en vais voir !

Dieuxième Damoiselle
Adieu, Meunier.

Meunier
              Jusqu'au revoir,
660   Ma damoiselle, grands mercis
Quelque bon jour, de sens rassis,[97]
Nous ferons chère plus meilleure.

Meunière
Vous en allez-vous à cette heure ?

Deuxième Damoiselle
664   Oui, je m'en vais mettre en la voie.

Meunière
Il vaut mieux que je vous convoie.

Deuxième Damoiselle
Je m'en irai toute seulette.

Meunier
Ah ! Il y a quelque belette
668   Ou bête avec ma poulaille.
Viens-t-en avec moi et me baille[98]
La palette de notre feu.

---

[97] *rassis*: calm.
[98] *baille*: to give.

Meunière

En avez-vous eu quelque peu
D'apercevance ?⁹⁹

Meunier

672   [143v] Oui, (comme) il me semble,
Car ils caquettent tous ensemble :
« Le fait entendu e[s]t compris ».

Premier Gentilhomme

C'est fait de nous, nous voilà pris.
676   Miséricorde, mes amis !

Meunier

Et qui, tous les diables, a mis
Ces galans-là parmi mes poules ?
Par la Mort bieu, si je ne bredouilles¹⁰⁰
680   Vos têtes a cette heure ici !

Premier Gentilhomme

Ah ! Monsieur le Meunier, merci !
Ayez pitié de nos personnes !

Meunière

Eh ! Ce sont nos deux Gentilshommes
684   Qui viennent céans pour gaber.¹⁰¹

Meunier

Ah, ils me veulent dérober !
Je soutiens la querelle à point !
Puisque je les tiens sur ce point :
688   Il vaut mieux que je les égorge !

Meunière

Et non ferez !

Meunier

               Vertu saint Georges !¹⁰²
Chacun d'eux ci a trop vécu.

Premier Gentilhomme

Vous avez cent et un écus
692   De moi, vraiment je vous les donne
Et de bon cœur vous en guerdonne
Et que de moi ne parlez plus.

---

[99] *apercevance* : a showing, a hint.
[100] *bredouiller vos têtes*: to smash the two heads together.
[101] *gaber*: to joke around.
[102] *saint Georges*: With the Miller holding the fire spit, the imagery is reminiscent of the saint's iconography where George kills the dragon with his lance.

####### Deuxième Gentilhomme
Et moi, de mes six-vingts Ph'lippus[103]
696 De ma monnaie et testons,[104]
Tout d'un accord nous soumettons
Vous en quitter et décharger.
Eh ! Nous voulez-vous laidenger ?[105]
700 Tous deux, vous demandons pardon.

####### Meunier
Me les donnez-vous à pur don ?

####### Premier Gentilhomme
Oui, sans jamais rien demander.

####### Deuxième Gentilhomme
Ce qu'il vous plaira commander
704 [144r] Nous le ferons à votre gré.

####### Meunier
Ci direz-vous, bon gré mal gré,
Combien que vous soyez fâchés,
Pourquoi vous êtes-vous cachés
708 Finement avec ma poulaille ?

####### Premier Gentilhomme
Crainte de vous.

####### Meunière
Eh, ne vous chaille…

####### Meunier
Taisez-vous, je les veux ouïr.

####### Deuxième Gentilhomme
Chacun de nous pensait jouïr
712 De votre femme follement.

####### Premier Gentilhomme
Vous avez eu bien finement
La jouïssance des deux nôtres.

####### Meunier
Par monsieur saint Thibaut l'apôtre,[106]
716 Contre vous deux aurai débat !

---

[103] On *Ph'lippus* see note 26.
[104] *testons*: from the italian *testone*, refering to the head of the sovereign found on one side. Currency created by Louis XII in 1514 and replaced by Henri III in 1576. In French, the word is evocative of *tétons*, breasts. The Second Gentleman, also engages in this wordplay, calling the Miller's Wife, *mon tétin*.
[105] *laidenger*: to hurt, to mistreat.
[106] *Saint Thibaut*: invoked by cuckolded husbands.

Deuxième Gentilhomme
Nous avons couroux pour ébat.

Premier Gentilhomme
Pour joie, avons mélancolie.

Meunier
[L'homme amoureux subit maint mat.]¹⁰⁷

Deuxième Gentilhomme
720   Nous avons couroux pour ébat

Meunier
Vous voilà donc pris au rabat,¹⁰⁸
Dont c'est à vous grosse folie.

Deuxième Gentilhomme
Nous avons couroux pour ébat.

Premier Gentilhomme
724   Pour joie, avons mélancolie.
      Quand Amour, un homme fol, lie,
      Il perd savoir et contenance.

Meunier
      Je prends congé de l'assistance.
728   Si peu que mon savoir contient
      Et dis pour toute récompense
      Qu'à trompeur, tromperie lui vient.
      [144v] Et pour réjouïr nos esprits
732   Une chanson, je vous supplie.

---

¹⁰⁷ We modified the hypermetric line *L'homme amoureux fait mainte folie* in order to construct a satisfying *rondeau triolet* (ABaAabAB). The word *mat* is found in *checkmate* and refers to the move by which the king is defeated.

¹⁰⁸ *être pris au rabat*: to be caught at the curb; the locution is taken from hunting with hounds.

The Farce of the Chicken Coop for Six Characters
(adapted into English verse)

The First Gentleman
Good day, to you Cousin.

Second Gentleman
                  Good day to you too!

First Gentleman
It's joyous to see you right here.
Your health, is it good? And your spirit is true?

Second Gentleman
4 By the grace of Our Lord, I've no fear!
I find nothing to fault, neither here nor yet there,
That vexes or causes me grief.

First Gentleman
Whoever contrives to give others despair
8 Should be banned like a dirty low thief!

Second Gentleman
Whoever imagines a foul evil plot,
And has planted it deep in his heart,
Deserves to be beaten right there on the spot!

First Gentleman
12 You always say things that sound smart!
Your speech, on all topics, has something to say.

Second Gentleman
As does yours!

First Gentleman
            Say no more, please, good sir...,
And how is the wife of our Miller today?

Second Gentleman
Who's that now?

First Gentleman

16   I dare say you know her!
But how I'd know her, I can't possibly guess,
Since you've already laid down your claim.
You scurry about as you haunt her address;
20   It's a wonder you live with the shame.
In the day and the night, in the morn and the eve,
We all hear your sweet Latin too well!
And you hunt for your prey in the trees and the leaves;
24   Aren't you frightened somebody will tell?
All your comings and goings add up, you must know,
Your sins are committed in view.
People see, and they note, and they wait for a show...

Second Gentleman

28   Dear Cousin, what is that to you?
It seems you've forgotten the truth of the case,
We've all seen you lurking 'round there.
People have told me that you're on the chase.
32   You've got nerve to reprove me unfair...ly.
You blame me, who is free of all evil thought?
I'm accused by your slanderous talk?
By you, who are worthy to be lined up and shot?
36   Take care you don't get a rude shock!
The truth will come out; it all will be known.

First Gentleman

And I'll wager whatever you care,
That you held her all naked, all bare to the bone!

Second Gentleman

40   And I'll double that bet if you dare!
I'll bet that you tossed her in bed on her ass!
By Our Lord, I will make you pay!
You watch yourself; I'll take none of your sass.

First Gentleman

44   Who has the best claim gets his way!
But let us not argue like quarrelsome guests,
We know the best tree by its fruit.
Good wine is selected by sav'ring sweetness...
48   From the depths of my heart I thus say, "May God bless";
Our shared meal should not make us dispute.

Miller's Wife enters Singing
There goes the Miller's Wife, There she goes, There goes the Miller's Wife...

Miller

You always find ways to sing without care;
52 By God, I dare not copy you.
Chaos would follow if that's how I'd fare,
Indeed, bedlam would join us here, too!
Instead, I must strive to make and unmake,
56 To come and to go... I feel cursed!
I feel like I'm falling apart for your sake:
You trollops can all do your worst!

Miller's Wife

What, pray God, is the matter?

Miller

                             I fear
60 That all will be lost, by high God.
I'm in court against someone who isn't sincere,
A low life, a liar, a fraud!
I wish that Our Lord put the hangman to work;
64 If he'd hanged I would like that right well!
But all at the court, from the judge to the clerk,
Yes... everyone thinks that he's swell!
His arrival is met with the best courtesies;
68 Those lawyers, they all love him there.
The sergeant of arms and the crass wannabees,
With both hands he grabs cash as they stare!

Miller's Wife

It will happen, eventually, one of these days,
72 You and I will go straight to that court.
We will speak with a voice, like you hear at the plays,
To the judges and their whole cohort.
If your opponent attacks me, then never you fear,
76 I'll know well how to handle that hood.
He will melt to the ground like a cheap racketeer;
All his law-talk will do him no good.

Miller

A case can't be brought without money, you know.
80 All trials are controlled by the devil!
He'll declare that I'm dead twenty years yet to go
'Til I'm sunk well below the street level.

Miller's Wife

There's nobody saying that you are dead yet!
84 Should you hang or impale yourself?
By the Mother of God, leave me to fret
How to quickly put cash on the shelf.

Miller
Did you say "cash"?

Miller's Wife
You heard me just fine!
88 There's no scheme that we can't contemplate.

Miller
Well, my belle dame, please tell me your mind:
Where's the money to help litigate?
It would please me so much if our case had a chance
92 With our wallet crammed full to the brim.
Twenty or thirty or forty, perchance?

Miller's Wife
At least fifty gold crowns we shall have in advance:
Each one red like the high Seraphim.
96 But we would be wise to not say a word;
On this matter we ought to have silence.

Miller
By gosh, you are right! I like what I've heard!
To get cash I'd even do violence.
100 Is there someone to target, or someone to mark
Against whom you have already plotted?

Miller's Wife
Our mill has two masters, each one a loan shark;
Of my body they're totally besotted.
104 If you feigned a long journey away from our home,
For a month, or twenty-some days,
We'd be weighed down with crowns. While you did roam
We could trick them in numerous ways.
108 And after the money is safe and secured
You can come home when you are pleased.
Sir Reynard the fox in his hole was assured
Next to them, once their money's been seized!
112 I think that they'll give us the rent on our mill,
And perhaps even all the arrears.
We've built up a debt that's as high as a hill,
And it buries us up to the ears.

Miller
116 God dammit, I think this a fine strategy!
But how can I act complicitly?

Miller's Wife
Go to bed, and I'll handle this plan craftily,
I'm well versèd in speaking illicitly.

First Gentleman [*entering*]

120 Why am I prevented from even one glance
At my Miller's delightful young wife?
Both the old and new law I would look at askance
And renounce them the rest of my life!
124 Zounds! If I could but hold her and keep her as mine
And have all my will and desire,
I would kiss her, oh, three by ten times
Whilst burning with amorous fire!
128 Oh! If I could but hold her on a soft feather bed
And ravish her for fifteen days…
That's it! I must travel now straight to her stead
My sorrow can brook no delays.
Hey, Miller!

Miller

132   For God's sake tell him I'm sleeping.
I'm tired and it's close to the truth!

Miller's Wife

God bless you, Sir!

First Gentleman

               …and hold you in safekeeping.
Will I get rent while I'm still in my youth?

Miller [*aside*]

136 I regret that we've not got your money today,
But "Whoever seeks money seeks trouble."

Miller's Wife

You've got a nerve to show up here this way
When his chin's not yet shaved of its stubble.

First Gentleman

140 It's early, I know; I'm half frozen with cold,
Won't you offer to help me get warm?
Why, just now I saw Death as this way I strolled,
By high God, 'twas a most chilling form.

Miller's Wife

144 Good sir! I think that it would be a stain on my soul
And a damnable infamous shame,
To be found having jumped into bed for a roll
And dishonour my husband's good name.

First Gentleman

148 Good lady, my heart bleeds profusely for you
And you're making me totally ill!
But if you are intent on refusing, just do!
I will turn and walk home from this mill.
152 But, by the pow'r of dread Death, I will work to ensure
That you both grow unhappy and dreary!

Miller's Wife

It can not be right now, and I must seem demure...
But first speak to my Lucas, my deary.
156 With him you'll advise on our case before court,
Honestly and secretly both,
For they plan to snatch, by a malicious tort
Our poor mill which is owned by an oath.
160 To cut to the chase and make long stories short
You must lend us the money we need.
And once we are settled, you can play and have sport.
Whatever you want I'll concede!

First Gentleman

164 Oh! Do you think me a miser who'd keep for my sake
Even one of those hundred doubloons?
Wake up, my Miller!

Miller's Wife

                 Yes, Lucas, please wake!
Will you sleep through the day until noon?

First Gentleman

168 There, there, my Miller! Let me give you my purse
It is full of gold coins, with quittance.

Miller

There is always someone who is acting adverse
And would harm me if given the chance.

Miller's Wife

172 Pay him no mind, he's still half asleep;
He's just having a terrible nap.
Your landlord, this noble (with pockets quite deep),
Wants to chat (so take off your cap!).
176 With a will that's quite free he brings us good news
So I thank this kind, generous man.
We were chatting of land, the home we might lose,
And the scoundrels who'd steal if they can.
180 He said it was foolish, and I think it's true,
To act in unvirtuous ways.
With one hundred crowns, or maybe two,
We'd be peaceful the rest of our days.

Miller

184 A... a.. hundred crowns? That's quite the large sum.
I think eighty would lessen the threat.
I've false letters to buy, and fine wines in the tun,
Backpayments, downpayments, and debt.
188 By my faith, when it comes to gold coins and accounts
I've only held very small piles!

First Gentleman

One hundred gold crowns is a weighty amount,
And, if taken, leads only to smiles.
Let me lend you the coin.

Miller

192   I'm already in debt!

First Gentleman

We'll just add to the total you owe.
But don't wait for too long, or I might just forget:
Make it sooner, not later, you go.
196 It's no trouble for me, those coins had been saved:
I was planning to make a downpayment.
Now, think to your business, the way has been paved:
Go become a victorious claimant.

Miller

200 A hundred gold crowns! That's more than I need
To settle the whole case completely!

First Gentleman

God be with you Miller.

Miller

                                 And to you Godspeed.

FIRST GENTLEMAN
And to you Dame.

MILLER'S WIFE
God keep you, discreetly.

FIRST GENTLEMAN
204 Please tell me, my dear, when should I return
So I can count down every minute?

MILLER'S WIFE
Once the Miller has gone, that's my main concern.
Shall we say five o'clock?

FIRST GENTLEMAN
That's my limit!
208 We must eat! I'll bring food, a delightful repast:
A roast capon beside a fat goose.

MILLER'S WIFE
And fine wine.

FIRST GENTLEMAN
Yes of course, we'll indulge to the last,
'Till our passions are finally let loose! [*exit First Gent.*]

MILLER
212 Look here, by Our Lord, I've got one hundred crowns!
One hundred gold crowns. Zounds, I love you!
You're the cream of all schemers, in cities or towns
The most subtle of all of them, too.

MILLER'S WIFE
216 You haven't seen anything yet, now be quiet.
Go back to your bed; look refreshed.
I am cunning enough for two men... Don't deny it!
[*enter Second Gent.*]
Here's the second who's easily threshed.
220 I've a plan, but be still and you'll hear as I try it,
Not a word and he'll soon be enmeshed.

SECOND GENTLEMAN
The love of a woman, it often deceives,
It tricks a man's heart every day.
224 I must race just as fast as the wind through the leaves
I am heartsick as I make my way.
I go to the Miller, whose Wife my heart grieves,
For her mercy I ever will pray.
228 I would tame her and hope that I gain some reprieves,
Or I surely will perish away.
I've one hundred one thousand most fond memories
Of her court'ous and courtly display!
Halloo! Miller.

MILLER'S WIFE
232   Tone it down, please!
Sir, your Miller is resting: go 'way.

SECOND GENTLEMAN
Oh, My dear bosom, my sweet love, my red rose,
Have I won you as yet to my will?
236 I've a heart that desires to achieve those sweet throes!
Listen now to the words I will spill...
Um, where's the Miller?

MILLER'S WIFE
        He's sleeping, good Sir.
He's really not cheery of late.

SECOND GENTLEMAN
What ails him?

MILLER'S WIFE
240   He simply prefers to defer,
So our debt is well past its due date.
Our debt on our homestead has risen so high
Our village estate's in arrears.
244 We pay one hundred francs, and that just scrapes by.
Just to tell of our woe beckons tears.
If we could but find an upright guarantor
Or somebody to lend against rent,
248 By my faith, that same hour we could eas'ly restore
Our inheritance, one hundred percent.
And then you would see him, the Miller I mean,
To skip like a cobbler with leather.

Second Gentleman

252 'Beg pardon, my lady, I mean nothing obscene,
Could we bring our two figures together?
Of Ph'lippus I'd lend you as much as six score,
With a hundred-some "sous" in spare change.

Miller's Wife

256 Alas, dear Sir, I dare not play the whore,
Or with husbands make such an exchange.

Second Gentleman

Alas, my dear Lady, I'm driven to madness
By love that has pushed me this way.
260 If it please you, allow me some joy and some gladness,
My fervid desire to allay.
In exchange I will give you, within the same hour,
Six score weighty "Ph'lippus" of gold,
264 With a hundred "sous tournois", a sizeable tower
Of money to have and to hold.

Miller's Wife

But at least, my dear Sir, you must swear to take keep
Of my honour, and also beware…

Second Gentleman

268 Not a word! I'll not come until all are asleep,
And we'll feast upon popish-like fare!

Miller's Wife

I accept!

Second Gentleman

Excellent! Now I'll speak to the Miller
To arrange about lending the money.

Miller's Wife

272 I'd have guessed, if I'd thought, that he'd be familiar
With the side of the bread that gets honey.

Second Gentleman

Oh Miller, wake up!

Miller's Wife

He's in a bad mood,
He's spent the whole day in a torpor.

Miller

276 You'll make my blood boil with that attitude!
Just the sound of your voice is like torture!

Miller's Wife

Poor dear, are you tired? Can you not lift your head?
It's not healthy to sleep all the time!
280 Come look, here's our lord, who quite boldly has said
That he wishes us pleasures sublime.
With a will that's quite free, he will lend us today
Six score "Ph'lippus" and one hundred "sous";
284 With all of that money our debt we'll repay;
Our lives will be free from abuse.

Miller

By St John! I pray God that he gives him long life
And keeps him in prosperity!

Second Gentleman

288 So, here you are Miller. It's all there, ask your wife.
Now see to your task ... with celerity.
Rest assured that in this I but follow my heart
(As I'm sure that you see it quite clearly),
292 Which willingly offers this loan to impart,
Though I usually don't lend cavalierly.
But you two, who presumably I might secure....
And what time do you leave? So I know...

Miller's Wife

296 My dear Sir, I would think him a boor and impure
If he waited ... or even went slow.

Miller

If that is the case then I'll leave right this minute
And I'll go without further delay.

Second Gentleman

300 So tell me, my sweet heart, when can we begin it?
When can we enjoy our soiree?

Miller's Wife

Well, I could squeeze you in for an hour after six,
Before seven, if that works for you?

Second Gentleman

304 I am far from afraid, I'd brave the dark Styx,
I can suffer the wait! Now, adieu!
You should arrange the space and tidy this place;
I'll return to collect what is due. [*exit Second Gent. and Miller's wife*]

MILLER

308 Lookie here! Lookie here! I've a fist full of gold!
　　Some women keep marv'lous accounts.
　　When dumb men do grow ears that their hats cannot hold
　　They *should* pay prepost'rous amounts.
312 But now to my business, what have I to do?
　　Primo, to vacate this place!
　　I'll leave them to talk for a minute or two,
　　'Till they start to draw close and embrace.
316 *Secondo*, to plan to be on my guard,
　　To keep a close eye on our guest.
　　The first one I catch in his subtle canard,
　　If he or my wife get undressed,
320 As soon as I see that he starts to act lewdly,
　　I'll instantly show him my mettle!

MILLER'S WIFE [*entering*]

　　I'd rather be dead than to suffer so rudely:
　　To have hands on my body to settle!
324 All I ask is you're careful to get here on time,
　　Your entrance cannot be too late.
　　For our good I engage in this foul pantomime;
　　We're agreed that you'll lie in await.

MILLER

328 Just leave it with me, it will all work out fine,
　　I think that you'll make some great bait. [*exeunt*]

FIRST GENTLEMAN [*entering*]

　　Will I soon be repaid for the hundred gold crowns
　　That I gave to the Miller, that knave?
332 Were it not for his wife, and her tight-fitting gowns,
　　He'd go penniless straight to his grave.
　　Except that her body my weak heart enflames,
　　So my spirit is almost expended.
336 But now is the time that she says and proclaims
　　That my miseries will fin'lly be ended.
　　And so I go there without fear or debate;
　　My love I'll no longer conceal!
　　Hey there, my sweetie!

MILLER'S WIFE [*entering*]
340 　　　　　　Who's there at the gate?

FIRST GENTLEMAN

　　It is I, come to finish our deal.

Miller's Wife

Your actions are courtly and so nonchalant;
I trust that you came without servants?

First Gentleman

344 What need do we have of a poor "poursuivant"
A third party would be a disturbance.
Let's taste the sweet wine and begin to relax
And then we will bite what we crave.

Miller

348 If you try to get close, make the beast with two backs,
My sweet lady, with *Monsieur le Brave*,
By God's death, I'd be forced to drive and to shove
My dagger deep into your breast!

First Gentleman

352 My heart does not want to be cured of your love,
When I think of you, dear, I'm obsessed!
At least not until your heart feels the same
And hopes to fulfill my desire.

Miller's Wife

356 Dear sir, over me you have a fair claim;
After supper I'll repay your hire.

First Gentleman

And where, my sweet pea, could your husband now be
In the time that he left this place?

Miller's Wife

At a good seven leagues?

First Gentleman

360   Good Lord, that's unlikely!

Miller's Wife

I think it's not far from the case!

Miller

Oh dear sir, Monsieur Butterfly-ette,
So you try to make me be the chump!?
364 I'll tie you up soon, or at least I will try it,
Or today I'll wind up in the dump.

First Gentleman

Let's drink this to you.

Miller's Wife

                         Well thank you, kind Sir!

Miller

The bargain will soon be completed.
368 We all know that *gallants*, with a debt to incur,
Never count, so they're easily cheated.

Second Gentleman [*entering*]

It is finally time! At long last I must go
To that woman who grants I-O-Us.
372 She agreed to our friendship, that I'll be her beau:
I'll collect as her interest accrues.
I suppose that she now is keenly preparing
Her hearth to receive me this night.
376 My blood is in turmoil, its wand'ring and erring
In despair, being out of her sight!
Open up! Open up!

Miller's Wife

            Who's that at the gate?

First Gentleman

Bloody Hell! I heard someone outside!
380 And now I am trapped without sword, or steel plate,
Or a dagger to safeguard my hide.

Second Gentleman

Good ev'ning! Good ev'ning!

Miller's Wife

                      I'll just get the door.

First Gentleman

Oh my God, my poor heart will give out!
384 I believe it's your husband! Christ grant me succour
Or my shame will be bandied about.

Miller's Wife

Then hide with the chickens, inside the small coop:
I'll call when he's gone at the last.

Second Gentleman

388 I squandered no time but I dashed to your stoop
As soon as the hour had passed.
This bottle is proffered, my sweet lady dear,
May I put it in its proper place.
392 It will properly pair the repast I brought here,
As an off'ring for mercy and grace.

Miller's Wife

Many thanks, my good sir, I've had time to prepare
A small banquet, so now we can share it.
396 Is there gossip to tell, or some news to lay bare,
That you know, Monsieur Cockschaffer-ette?

Miller

Gossip? Monsieur Butterflyette, as nobody knows,
Is now sitting right next to our chicken.
400 Even now, as he roosts, he will twist his *huevos*;
In that coop he is stringently stricken.

First Gentleman

All the devils of Hell, who would have guessed?
Look at Monsieur Cockschaffer-ette:
404 "It's a dirty lewd bird that will foul his own nest":
Well, I'm gobsmacked! I just cannot bear it!
The next time this happens I will be much wiser;
I'll be sure to keep one eye behind!

Second Gentleman

408 Oh, my sister, allow me to play the adviser:
We should drink a full glass and unwind.

First Gentleman

Bloody Hell, he's a villain, a scoundrel, a bounder!
Drinks *my* wine and eats *my* bread!?
412 I'm just speechless! I'm dumbstruck! My words they just founder!
I have to get out of this shed!
Then this game of desire will enhance his disgrace!

Second Gentleman

Let's lie down just behind this long blind;
416 Then our game of sweet love will continue apace.

Miller's Wife

No, not yet!

Miller

    I am watching your kind!
Monsieur Cockschafferette, what are you doing?
That's surely no way to behave!
420 Coming into my house and my wife pursuing!

Second Gentleman

My dear lady, your mercy I crave!
When will I be freed of my long-suff'ring pain?

Miller's Wife
After supper: then take me bodily.
424 You'll do as you want, all your pleasures attain,
But for now, we will talk... a bit naughtily. [*they draw close*]
Just seeing you causes my heart to rejoice.

Miller
Ah! I can't suffer this one minute more!
428 I am losing my senses, my mind, and my voice...
Dagnabbit! I'll go through that door!
This is killing me, forced to watch how she dotes;
I will act like I've drunken my fill.
432 Bloody Hell, When I get there I could slit their throats....
Open up! Open up!

Miller's Wife
Keep still!
What is it that moves you to such agitation?

Second Gentleman
I think that's our Miller I hear!
436 Jesus Christ, say goodbye to my good reputation.

Miller's Wife
Oh Jesus!

Second Gentleman
I called Him in fear.
May He help me to flee and escape from this place!

Miller's Wife
Quickly, throw yourself right in to there...
440 There, with the chickens, in the coop – there is space –
My husband's quite jealous ... beware,
If he found you, he'd kill you with no thought of the cost.

First Gentleman
You've arrived at the end of your game,
444 In a coop, with the chickens, in disgrace, we both lost.

Miller
At the top of my voice I proclaim:
I will break down this door if you keep it closed!

Miller's Wife
My God, what a noisy display!
448 I've not seen a person so drunk'ly disposed!

Miller
Lord, I'm hungry! Get out of my way!

Second Gentleman
Well there goes our dinner, I commit it to God!
For it shortly will be all devoured.

Miller
452 So tell me, my deary, my sweet golden bawd,
What have you prepared us this hour?

Miller's Wife
Sit down and relax, you can certainly see
We have lots of good food from the kitchen.
456 Here you have stew, a ham fricassee,
Partridges, wine, bread and pidgeon.

First Gentleman
Well that does it, we're completely depleted.
May all devels take drunkards to Hell!

Miller
460 Just sav'ring fine wine makes my blood awfully heated,
And this supper's most warming as well.
That lovely young woman, could you fetch her for me?
Madame de Butterflyette?
464 Please tell her I'd like her to join me for tea,
And not to worry if she didn't eat yet.

Miller's Wife
I will go straight away.

Miller
                              But my dear please be sure
Not to dawdle but bring her in haste.

First Gentleman
468 Why that villain will kill me if his plan is impure,
He's sent for my wife, who is chaste!
If this news gets around, or if anyone knows,
I'll ensure that that man is enlisted!

Second Gentleman
472 If he hears us discussing (so speak through your nose)
He'll ensure that our necks are all twisted!

Miller *singing*
Ho! Drink up! Drink up!
Again and again and again!
476 *Ho! Drink up! Drink up!*
To the sound of a clarion!

FIRST GENTLEMAN
Does he really believe that we find all this droll:
This fine singing that brings no delight?
480   I'd dance with no pleasure, trapped in this hole.
May God curse your fat gut's appetite!

MILLER'S WIFE [*arriving before the First Lady*]
I hope you don't mind that I've come here to you
Not receiving a solicitation.
484   To my dear lady friend, my husband so true,
My Lucas, sends this invitation.
He begs to you now, on account of great love,
That you will accompany me...

FIRST LADY
And where to, madam?

MILLER'S WIFE
488   Well with me... sort of,
To laugh and rejoice... mutually.

FIRST LADY
I'd not dare go with you.

MILLER'S WIFE
                          Why would you say that?
Ah! I see! There is nothing to fear.
492   You'll forget all your sorrows, with no caveat,
Once the words of the Miller you hear.

FIRST LADY
Alright, let us go, but you have to beware
That I can't linger long over dinner.
496   If my husband, my master, if he found me there
I'd be scorned as a damnable sinner.

MILLER'S WIFE
I won't be so foolish – you needn't dismay –
I wouldn't allow you to dither.

FIRST LADY
Good evening, my Miller.

MILLER
500   Good day, good day
Ah, young lady, won't you please come hither.

MILLER'S WIFE
Please come right in, sit yourself on this seat
So that you can be at your ease.

FIRST LADY
Many thanks.

MILLER'S WIFE
504   It's my pleasure, sincerely a treat.

FIRST LADY
Miller! Stop!

FIRST GENTLEMAN
        That cad just gave her a squeeze!
That nasty small man, what will he do next?

SECOND GENTLEMAN
God dammit, you must be discreet!
508 We must sit and be quiet and bear these hen-pecks!

MILLER
Can I send you again down the street?
I would like you to fetch Madame Cockschafferette.
She should join us here for our fine feast.
512 I desire her presence, or I'll be upset.

FIRST LADY
You're a dutiful liege, at the least,
But your services go beyond right at this time!

MILLER
My young lady, I'll just drink to you.

FIRST LADY
516 Oh dear Sir, I'll say "Thanks", knowing that's not a crime.

FIRST GENTLEMAN
May a sword pierce your heart through and through!
Such sorrows you cause! They are too much to bear!

MILLER
May I now ask about something that's lewd?
520 Can you guess what I'm thinking, my lady so fair?

FIRST LADY
What is it you think?

MILLER
        By the Rood...
The thought, it occurs, and I would like to know,
If I tried to entice you to kiss,
524 Is that something you'd do, or would you say "no"?

FIRST LADY
You're certainly not doing this!
We'd simply not dare, or at least not in here...

MILLER
And why not?

FIRST LADY
It's offensive to God!

MILLER
528   Offensive to God!? Oh, we've nothing to fear!
Do you think no one else is a bawd?
Oh, please let me have just one *amuse bouche*.

FIRST GENTLEMAN
Oh, please let her give him a slap!
532   That traitor, foul leper, that seedy Scaramoch!

SECOND GENTLEMAN
For the very last time, shut your trap!
Gosh darnit! Shut up! Don't say even one word!
If this drunkard should happen to hear us,
536   (Although now his advances they go undeterred),
By St. Blaise, he could very well spear us!
He'd kill us and our deaths would be known, infamous.

FIRST GENTLEMAN
But he's trying to screw my pure wife!

SECOND GENTLEMAN
540   So what? You're losing a thing that is just ... frivolous.

FIRST GENTLEMAN
If he hanged, that would lessen my strife:
Oh, may God and the beautiful Mary be witness!

MILLER
My young lady, shall we start our play?
544   It is the best way to be cured of our sickness.

FIRST LADY
Just don't tell my husband, OK?

MILLER
I would rather be damned than to have us revealed!
Let us enter the lists uncontrolled;
548   Like a chivalrous knight I will pierce your strong shield!

FIRST GENTLEMAN
Well, that's it. I am now a cuckold.
The dolorous fate of poor husbands is sealed!

SECOND GENTLEMAN
One betrayed and both hurt, the two left on the field!

FIRST GENTLEMAN
552 Rest assured, that his death's been foretold!

MILLER'S WIFE [*arriving before the Second Lady*]
Good day, gracious Lady! I've come all this way
Just to see you and make a proposal:
My dear husband was hoping you'd share his buffet
556 And thus put yourself at his disposal.

SECOND LADY
I don't know how I'd ever repay such respect,
For giving me such fulsome service.

MILLER'S WIFE
But in truth, my dear lady, he said, in effect,
560 You must come or you would make him nervous.

SECOND LADY
Well, in that case my duty I will not neglect:
I'll make good if the saint's will preserve us.

FIRST GENTLEMAN
Who would have thought, by the devils in Hell,
564 That she'd suffer this putrid... incident?
That this dirty, foul villain could eas'ly compel
My chaste wife to release her sweet instrument?
The traitor, I still hear him grunting! The swine!
568 He makes me wear horns on my cap.

MILLER
Did I hurt you?

FIRST LADY
       No, no! I am just fine!

FIRST GENTLEMAN
I hope you come down with the clap!

SECOND GENTLEMAN
Alas, you must grin as you drink this foul brew,
572 And so suffer the pain in your heart.

FIRST LADY
You promised to see that my honour stays true:
I trust that you'll now play your part.

SECOND LADY [*entering*]
Good ev'ning, my Miller.

MILLER
                              Good ev'ning madam.
576   You are certainly welcome right here!
Well, it seems I'll indulge in a second fine dram
Of that wine. So I'll drink to your cheer!

MILLER'S WIFE
Oh my lady, has something gone wrong or awry?
580   You suddenly seem quite unsettled.

FIRST LADY
Alas, I've grown weary, I don't know whereby,
But this house has me feeling bedeviled.

MILLER
Could you take her back home; you can see she's upset.

MILLER'S WIFE
I'll do that with pleasure.

FIRST LADY
584   Let's go.

MILLER
Good ev'ning again, Madame Cockschafferette,
Just seeing you makes my joy grow.

SECOND LADY
It seems that my journey's been lucky today.
588   Look: fine bread, full plates and sweet wine!

MILLER
For these last four months I've been meaning to say
That I want to invite you to dine.

SECOND LADY
Well, thank you, kind sir.

MILLER
                              Weren't you one of our guests
592   In our mill, five days having receded?
And while you were with us, your linen-white breasts,
Being dusted with flour, weren't they kneaded?

Second Lady
That my body was fondled, by you, I'll admit,
596 But I didn't allow you to linger!

Miller
But it was was quite close, by holy writ,
That I found your locked door with my finger.
But unfortunately, we were watched from behind,
600 Or our legs would have been interlaced.

Second Gentleman
Bloody Hell, he's insulting! We're being maligned!
Such rude talk with my wife is misplaced!

First Gentleman
Do you honestly think that he will shy away
604 From treating your wife as was mine?
May my body be put in hot metal today
If he fails her! Oh, now I feel fine!

Miller
My young lady, I beg you deny yourself nothing
608 Eat and drink 'til your heart is content!

Second Lady
The sweet talk of you Millers will soon have me blushing,
You speak nothing but shrewd argument.

Second Gentleman
What is she saying!? Shut up silly cow!
612 You're flirting with that stupid turd!?

Miller
If I only had sight of your *belle-chose* now
Methinks I would be fully cured.
But I only desire to compare what you've got
616 With what's hidden 'tween my wife's long legs.

First Gentleman
Oh, just listen to him butting in with that rot;
To whomever will listen he begs.
And all is to get what he wants from these women!

Second Gentleman
620 He's a cad! The proof's in the pudding!
I'm so helpless and angry my head is just swimmin';
I don't know which way to be looking!

####### Miller
My dear love, are you happy refusing my prayer,
624   And leaving me drained of my vigour?

####### First Gentleman
The worse it's for you; all these depths of despair
Come from aping a piteous figure!

####### Miller
My dear love, will you leave me deferred and suspended,
628   In misery and wretched calamity?

####### Second Lady
But I fear that our tryst might someday be presented
To my husband, wherever that *he* might be.
If the day ever came, on which he found out,
632   He would hold it against me perpetually.

####### Miller
May the devil take gossips who whisper about!

####### Second Lady
I will have to accept you, eventually!

####### Second Gentleman
Oh dear Mother Mary, your mercy I crave!
636   That scoundrel is banging my precious!

####### First Gentleman
Oh my God! Stop your wailing; you have to behave!
Or I'll squeeze you and leave you quite breathless!
He logged a full hour in bed with my poppet,
640   And through it you kept me all gagged!

####### Second Gentleman
But he's groping her!

####### First Gentleman
                    Do you think you can stop it?
He's the devil! His strength has not flagged.

####### Second Gentleman
All the saints and my friends, I beg for your grace!
644   Ugh...in chorus he pants and he farts!
And I'm forced to stand here, in this filthy place,
While he fondles my wife's private parts!

####### First Gentleman
Oh dear God! Do you want to make sure that we're killed!
648   I command that you shut up this instant!

SECOND GENTLEMAN
By Christ's death, that commandment will go unfulfilled!

FIRST GENTLEMAN
I'm afraid that I must be insistent. [*they struggle*]
And why should you not? For I was kept quiet!

SECOND GENTLEMAN
Murder!

FIRST GENTLEMAN
Oh, help!

SECOND GENTLEMAN
652   How should I behave?

FIRST GENTLEMAN
You should stuff it!

SECOND GENTLEMAN
                    But I'd rather die in a riot!
Help! Someone! I'm slain by this knave!

FIRST GENTLEMAN
What are you doing? You screamed like the dickens!

SECOND GENTLEMAN
656 'Cause you wrenched at my family jewels!

MILLER
There's somebody hiding out there with the chickens,
Gosh darnit, I'll see to those fools.

SECOND LADY
God bless you, my Miller.

MILLER
                    'Till we meet again,
660 My lady, I thank you sincerely.
On some other day, that Our Lord will ordain,
We will once again feast cavalierly.

MILLER'S WIFE [*entering*]
My Lady, I see that you're leaving already?

SECOND LADY
664 Yes, madam, I must make my way.

MILLER'S WIFE
Shall I walk with you, Lady, to help keep you steady?

SECOND LADY
No, thank you, I simply can't stay. [*exit Second Lady*]

MILLER
Listen…, There's a weasel, I think, or some other beast
668   With our chickens outside in the coop.
But come with me now and he'll soon be deceased…
Get the spit from the fire … and the scoop.

MILLER'S WIFE
What is it, my husband, do you see a critter,
Or several?

MILLER
672   They seem to be near.
They are bustling together: Oh how they chitter!
"That's most true which we least care to hear."

THE FIRST GENTLEMAN
That's it! We're done for! And now we've been caught.
676   I beg for your mercy, my friends!

MILLER
How the Hell did we end in this Gordian knot,
With these popinjays amongst my hens?
By the blood of Our Lord I should pluck that long hair
680   From both of your heads right this moment.

FIRST GENTLEMAN
Ah! Miller, kind sir, please have mercy, take care,
Have pity: we'll offer atonement.

MILLER'S WIFE
Aren't those the two nobles in business with us?
684   They wanted to play a small jest!

MILLER
No! They wanted to rob me, or raise a big fuss:
But I'm ready to face this unrest.
Since I find myself here with a clear upper hand,
688   It is right that I should cut your gullet.

MILLER'S WIFE
That is *not* in the right!

MILLER
                    By St George, understand:
When your flock is too large you should cull it!

First Gentleman
I've already lent you one hundred gold crowns,
692   I give them to you open handed,
You can have them now freely to spend in the towns,
We'll call it a gift that's been granted.

Second Gentleman
And me, the six score Ph'lippus I'll give:
696   It's been counted in coins big and small.
On the record I say it: this debt I forgive.
They're all yours whatever befall.
Despite all of that, you'd still see us abused?
700   We two, who beg for deliverance?

Miller
Are you giving me gifts, with debts all excused?

First Gentleman
Yes truly; without let or hindrance.

Second Gentleman
And whatever you wish to demand that we do,
704   We'll do as you wish right this minute.

Miller
Whether you wish it or not, I wish that I knew
What might anger you now to admit it.
What I'd like to know is how that you got here:
708   Furtively among my chickens.

First Gentleman
We were hiding in fear!

Miller's Wife
              Why ask that, my dear?

Miller
Listen up, as the sauce slowly thickens.

Second Gentleman
We both thought that we could contract an exchange
712   For the services your wife had to offer.

First Gentleman
But instead it is you who, with cunning, arranged
To take privileges our wives did proffer.

Miller
By the holy apostle, we call St Thibaut,
716   You both should be knocked on your arse to and fro.

SECOND GENTLEMAN
We sought only joy but we got only woe.

FIRST GENTLEMAN
We wanted some fun but are haunted by pain.

MILLER
The man who's in love will receive *quid pro quo*.

SECOND GENTLEMAN
720   We sought only joy but we got only woe.

MILLER
Now you are trapped here with nowhere to go,
'Cause your plan, it was downright insane.

SECOND GENTLEMAN
We sought only joy but we got only woe.

FIRST GENTLEMAN
724   We wanted some fun but are haunted by pain.
When a man starts to love he corrodes his own brain:
And he loses both reason and wit.

MILLER
I agree, but it's time now we quit: [*to the audience*]
728   To you, from my schooling, this maxim I'll leave
And I say it for our benefit:
When he deceives, it's deception he'll receive.
And so, to rejoice our spirit
732   I pray that a song we'll submit. [*They sing.*]

Contributor Biographies

Andrew Bretz is an adjunct instructor at Wilfrid Laurier University, McMaster University, the University of Guelph and Brock University, specializing in early modern poetry and drama. He has previously been published in *Modern Philology, Notes and Queries,* and *ESC* and has a chapter in *OuterSpeares: Shakespeare, Intermedia and the Limits of Adaptation*, edited by Daniel Fischlin (Toronto, 2014). He is preparing a book from his post-doctoral research with the *Canadian Adaptations of Shakespeare Project*.

Marla Carlson is Associate Professor in the Department of Theatre and Film Studies at the University of Georgia. Publications on medieval performance include *Performing Bodies in Pain: Medieval and Post-Modern Martyrs, Mystics, and Artists* (Palgrave, 2010) and "*Le Mystère de Saint Sébastien's* Villain: 'No Cuckoo is a Sparrowhawk,'" in *Les Mystères* (Rodopi, 2012). She is completing *Affect, Animals, and Autists: Feeling Around the Edges of the "Human" in Performance*.

Kirsten Inglis teaches Renaissance and seventeenth-century literature in the Department of English at the University of Calgary. Her research has been published in the journal *Early Theatre; Editing, Performance, Texts: New Practices in Medieval and Early Modern English Drama* (Palgrave, 2014); and most recently in *Food and Theatre on the World Stage* (Routledge, 2015). She is currently working on a monograph on Tudor women's translations and the politics of early modern gift culture.

Alexandra F. Johnston is professor emerita in the Department of English at the University of Toronto. She was the founding Director of *Records of Early English Drama* and remains involved in the project. Her third REED collection, the *Records of Berkshire* has been submitted for the checking process by the REED staff. A selection of her articles on medieval drama is forthcoming from Ashgate in 2016.

Mario Longtin is Associate Professor of French at Western University and chief editor of ROMARD. He is a medievalist, a philologist and an historian of theatre. He is currently co-editing a 16th-century manuscript from Rouen containing 74 play-texts with a team of international scholars. The collaboration with Richard Moll found in this volume is one of the first fruits of this venture. For ten years, he has also served as the artistic director of *Le Théâtre L'On Donne* in London.

Richard J. Moll completed his graduate work at the Center for Medieval Studies (University of Toronto) and is currently Associate Professor of English at Western University, Ontario. He is the editor of William Caxton's *Booke of Ovyde named Methamorphose* (Toronto and Oxford, 2013) and the author of *Before Malory: Reading Arthur in Later Medieval England* (Toronto, 2003) and articles on British romance, heraldry and historiography.

Dimitry Senyshyn is a PhD candidate at the University of Toronto. He has co-edited an old-spelling edition of *The True Tragedie of Richard the Third* for QME and the Internet Shakespeare Editions and is currently co-editing a modern-spelling edition of *Sir Clyomon and Sir Clamydes*. He contributed to the preparation of the REED *Inns of Court* volume, and he has published in *Theatre Research in Canada*, *Early Theatre*, and the *Encyclopedia of the Bible and its Reception*.

Charlotte Steenbrugge is a Marie Curie Research Fellow, funded by the European Commission Research Executive Agency to research the connections between sermons and drama in late medieval England at the Universities of Toronto (Canada) and Bristol (UK). She has published on English, Dutch, and French drama, including a monograph *Staging Vice: A Study of Dramatic Traditions in Medieval and Sixteenth-Century England and the Low Countries* (Brill / Rodopi, 2014).

Erin Weinberg is a PhD candidate at Queen's University in Kingston, Ontario, working on affect in Shakespeare's comedies. Her research interests include early modern affect, trauma, and the role of food in literature. She has published in the *Shakespeare Institute Review* (2012) and has an article forthcoming in *Pacific Coast Philology*.

www.ingramcontent.com/pod-product-compliance
Lightning Source LLC
Chambersburg PA
CBHW050110170426
43198CB00014B/2527